Praise for *Minu*

"Joanne Moody's book, *Minute by Minute*, is the story of a most amazing testimony of healing. It's one of the greatest healings I have seen, and one of the most documented histories of pain and disability. But, it is not just the story of her healing; it is the story of living life with disabling pain for years, and life after healing. It includes an out of body experience at her death. This is an amazing book, one that I highly recommend to everyone."

—RANDY CLARK, D. MIN. TH.D., INTERNATIONAL SPEAKER, FOUNDER AND PRESIDENT OF GLOBAL AWAKENING

"Powerful, inspiring, and refreshing! Joanne's testimony gives hope and encouragement to those whose healing hasn't come yet and inspires them to not give up, but to continue to press into a holy pursuit of a healing touch from God. The testimony of years of excruciating pain testifies of the grace of God that she encountered daily as God supplied all she needed each day. The testimony of healing cries out to the Lord to do it again! It creates a passion to experience more of the power and presence of the Lord. Read this book and be inspired!"

—RODNEY HOGUE, INTERNATIONAL SPEAKER

"Having watched both the debilitating illness in Joanne's life and her miraculous healing, her story is a living epistle of what God desires for each of us. The Father longs to heal, restore, and commission us to represent His heart to a world and Church struggling to believe Christ's death offers both forgiveness and healing." (Psalm 103:2–5)

—FRANCIS ANFUSO, AUTHOR AND FEATURED SPEAKER, K-LOVE CHRISTIAN RADIO

"Joanne is a truly gifted writer. Her story is engaging and honest. She creates great word pictures and honest responses. Joanne's description of God is the God we all want to know!"

—BLAINE COOK, INTERNATIONAL SPEAKER

Minute
by
Minute

Minute by Minute

A Pivotal Question *from* God, My Response, *and the* Remarkable Miracles That Followed

Joanne Moody

EMANATE
BOOKS

Published in Nashville, Tennessee, by Emanate Books, an imprint of Thomas Nelson. Emanate Books and Thomas Nelson are registered trademarks of HarperCollins Christian Publishing, Inc.

Thomas Nelson titles may be purchased in bulk for educational, business, fund-raising, or sales promotional use. For information, please e-mail SpecialMarkets@ThomasNelson.com.

Author's disclaimer: I have tried to recreate events, locales, and conversations from my memories and my journals. To maintain their anonymity, in some instances I have changed the names of individuals and places. I also have changed some of the identifying characteristics and details such as physical properties, places of residence, and medical care facilities.

ISBN 978-0-7852-1614-8 (TP)

ISBN 978-0-7852-1730-5 (eBook)

Library of Congress Control Number: 2017943896

Printed in the United States of America

For Mike and Kian,
the loves of my life, and
Jesus Christ, my everything

Contents

Contents

Foreword

Joanne anguished in pain at a level too intense to imagine for fourteen years. Not even the strongest pain medications gave her relief. I cried through the accounts of her tortured life. I have to wonder how she maintained the will to keep pressing forward. Amazingly, however, even when she wasn't experiencing healing for herself, she still prayed with faith for other people's healing. In spite of the unimaginable trials that Joanne endured night and day, she still maintained her belief that God is good, God is love, and that God heals.

When God highlighted Joanne to me at the VOA conference in Orlando, Florida, in August 2013, I casually prayed for her in obedience to His nudging as I passed by her. Then as I returned to my seat, I realized God had something big in mind. I went back to where she was on the floor, the most comfortable position for her as the pain was very intense.

I asked if I could pray again and the Holy Spirit took over. God had set up yet another divine appointment. Joanne's total and miraculous healing was the result! Yea God!

When God blows His breath on us, what we become is rarely what we can imagine or dream. He changes our direction and we dedicate our lives to His calling, and it becomes our main purpose. Joanne's healing sparked a compelling passion to listen to the Holy Spirit, pray, and see God heal.

Bill Johnson says that God gives breakthrough in personal experience so we will use the elevated position of favor to equip the saints. The healing Joanne received has elevated her to a place of favor in an amazing way. She is an atmosphere changer in God's kingdom—bringing heaven to earth everywhere she goes. It is her relentless desire to teach and share her testimony so that all the saints are equipped to pray for the sick and see people gloriously healed by the power of the Holy Spirit.

I am deeply humbled to know this mighty woman of God. As you read the pages of her book, I pray that you also will be compelled to pray for the sick and declare that the impossible is nothing for God.

RICHARD HOLCOMB
Global Awakening Board of Directors
Impact Christian Fellowship, Kerrville,
Texas, Core Leadership Team
Real Estate Developer

1

The Birth of More
than a Baby

I have two problems with hard labor: hard and labor.
I prefer soft, and I'd prefer not giving birth.

—JAROD KINTZ, AUTHOR

alf the city of Redondo Beach, California, was pregnant
that cold, overcast day in January 1999. That could be a
slight exaggeration, but when my husband, Mike, and I arrived
at the hospital, the corridors were crammed with women in
all stages of labor. There had been no power outages, no snow-
storms, nothing to explain the baby boom we were witnessing.
I was dressed in the largest clothes I owned—extra-large men's
gray sweatpants and a flowing, multicolored flowered tunic—
and yet, I still felt like a sausage crammed into its casing. I wore
black wool clogs one size larger than usual to accommodate my
swollen feet. My normally small frame was stretched to bursting.

I took my seat in the offered wheelchair, and a harried nurse wheeled me into a labor-delivery prep area. With hurried efficiency, she hooked me up to an external fetal heart-rate monitor.

"Your contractions are still five minutes apart, but there's no dilation yet. I'll let your doctor know you're here," she said, before rushing out of the room.

I had suffered a miscarriage a few months before this pregnancy, but that didn't diminish my hope for the birth of this child. Mike held my hand as another contraction hit. The nurse returned a few minutes later to inform us that Dr. Smith, my obstetrician, was out of town for a family emergency. His partner, Dr. Fletcher, would handle my delivery.

"I've called Dr. Fletcher and I'm waiting to hear back from her." The nurse smiled as she left the room, but that did nothing to lessen the fear gripping my stomach.

"I knew it!" I said to Mike, as a wave of uneasiness gripped me. The back of my throat constricted against the verbal and physical bile threatening to escape.

Twice during my pregnancy, Dr. Fletcher had examined me when Dr. Smith was unavailable. She had been reluctant to interact any more than absolutely necessary. During each of the two office visits, Dr. Fletcher had been unwilling to meet my gaze, her speech had been terse, and her manner impersonal. She seemed to lack even a shred of empathy, and any details I provided about my pregnancy challenges were disregarded. I couldn't understand why she had chosen to bring babies into the world.

After my second exam by Dr. Fletcher, I called my mom.

"Hi, Mom."

"Hey! How are you feeling?"

"I just came back from the obstetrician, and I saw Dr. Smith's partner. She is the most unfeeling, heartless doctor I have ever met. I just know I am going to have her when it's time for my baby to come."

"That's ridiculous, Joanne. Your doctor will be there to deliver your baby. But I still don't understand why you're insisting on a natural childbirth with all the birthing problems in our family. Why can't you just have a C-section and not go through all that?" (My mom warned me throughout my pregnancy: "Most females in our family don't fully dilate. You need to ask for a C-section.")

"They aren't going to just give me a C-section, Mom! I'm in good shape. I'll be strong enough to do this. I told my doctor about our family history, so he is prepared to do a C-section if I need one. I can do this. Plus, I've been told natural childbirth is better for the baby."

"Oh, brother! Bev and Patty were pulled out with forceps, and you and Dave were C-sections. All four of you turned out fine!"

Somehow this wasn't comforting. Forceps grasping and extracting my child from my body was not a birthing method I wanted to partake in. I had been in peak condition as a body builder and runner for more than twenty years. I was disciplined and had the stamina to endure extreme physical demands. Why would childbirth be any different? Besides, we were praying and had a host of friends praying too.

My mom didn't relent. "People are nuts telling you all this stuff, Joanne. Don't you remember the trouble Patty had with her kids? She labored forever with Jill and then ripped from stem to stern when the baby crowned. She had to have a C-section with Brian."

"It'll be all right, Mom. I'm not tiny like Patty. I am big-boned, sturdy Miles stock. Patty is married to six-foot-four-inch

Mark, and her babies were bound to be big. As long as I don't get Dr. Fletcher, everything will work out."

"Well, have Mike call me the minute the baby is born, and I'll be on the next flight. I'm not coming out until he is born."

"Okay. I wish you would come earlier, but I get it. Do what works for you, and I'll see you when he's here," I said and hung up.

It was disconcerting that my mom refused to come until after our son was born. Was it because she didn't want to witness any struggles I might have? The conversation unsettled me. I shoved doubt away like overcooked broccoli because I was a glass-half-full person. The misgivings Mom expressed about my ability to give birth got under my skin. Usually upbeat and positive, she was adamant that her daughters would struggle in childbirth.

To shake the dark feeling, I gave myself a pep talk and dismissed my mother's concerns. I put the conversation firmly out of my mind and concentrated on the task ahead. I would beat the odds. I would be the first in my family to have a baby naturally without incident.

The nurse returned a few minutes later to tell us Dr. Fletcher had called and was sending us home because my labor hadn't advanced. The confused look on Mike's face mirrored my own.

"Are you sure?" Desperation tinged my voice. "I'm in a lot of pain, and my contractions are five minutes apart. I can't go home." If begging would help, I'd do it.

The nurse began to unhook the monitor. "I would let you stay if I had the authority, Mrs. Moody, but there's nothing we can do until Dr. Fletcher formally admits you. Don't worry, this happens a lot." She gave us a reassuring smile and left the room.

Throughout my pregnancy, I was persistent in telling my doctor how necessary it was for him to be there for the birth of my baby. I never explained how much I disliked his partner—confrontation is not my strong suit. I didn't want to insult his choice of colleagues but tried to gain his commitment that there would be no possibility Dr. Fletcher would be in charge of my delivery. Each time I brought it up, Dr. Smith gave me a squeeze on the shoulder and assured me he would be the attending physician. What irony to be in the very situation I had desperately sought to avoid!

Mike helped me to the car, and we drove home. I headed to bed in total agony that lasted for the rest of the day. Mike called the hospital early that evening, but a nurse said we shouldn't return until the contractions were three minutes apart. My contractions intensified, but they weren't consistent. *What is going on? This isn't how it's supposed to go!* My heart raced, and I couldn't find any rhythm to my labor. We had learned the rhythm of labor in our birthing classes, and mine was all wrong. Finally, Mike drove me back to the hospital and demanded they admit me. It was 11:45 p.m.

The chaos of the overflowing obstetrics wing had only increased. The cries of laboring women echoed down the hallway while the pandemonium of my own labor pain matched the atmosphere around me. The night nurse came to check the Doppler fetal monitor and to give me an injection of Nubain, a synthetic analgesic that helps take the edge off labor pains. I am allergic to some narcotics—and highly sensitive to most—but the nurse assured me that Nubain would not make me nauseous.

I gasped as another set of contractions forced me upright. The monitor indicated the contractions were peaking, but I still had not dilated. I shouldn't have been surprised because of the lack of dilation in our family history, but I simply couldn't accept that things weren't progressing normally. It made no sense to me

2

Muscle and Music

I ran and ran and ran every day, and I acquired this
sense of determination, this sense of spirit that I would
never, never give up, no matter what else happened.

—WILMA RUDOLPH, OLYMPIC GOLD MEDAL WINNER

Come on, you guys! Keep up the pace!" I turned, panting, to my friends who were trailing thirty yards behind me. It was six o'clock, and the morning sun was just rising over the top of the Pali Highway. Our small group of runners was trying to make it to the other side of Kailua before stop-start morning traffic took to the streets. "At this rate we won't make it back in time for dinner." I laughed as Rox glared at me from behind.

It was Christmas Day 1993. I had just started a new holiday tradition of running across the island of Oahu via the Pali Highway from Kailua to downtown Honolulu, a daunting sixteen miles. In the best shape of my life, I had convinced four of my friends to join me on the run. In honor of the day, I had persuaded them to wear red long underwear with "Merry Fitness" embroidered across the rear. We completed our holiday running ensembles with oversized Santa hats and blinking battery-operated lights strung around our necks. With my family living on the mainland, I had nothing better to do that day.

Standing in my front yard earlier that morning, we kicked off our inaugural holiday run with the singing of "The Star-Spangled Banner." I'm sure my neighbors loved it. At 5:15, in the predawn darkness, we set out at an easy pace.

In an extraordinary display of planning, two other friends, Rocky and Ian, drove a red pickup truck to bring us water at designated points along the way. I had included an incentive package in the invitation to participate in the morning's festivities—a huge Christmas dinner when we finished. Bonded by friendship and without family for the holidays, we ran with determination to push our bodies to the limit.

Most of us were musicians, and the music that blared from the water truck that followed us kept us focused and motivated. Unfortunately, Rocky and Ian quickly tired of our slow pace and decided to find a convenience store and grab some snacks while we continued running.

Without our motivational music we struggled to keep our groove, going up the Pali Highway proved more challenging than we had anticipated. The long, steep grade up the Ko'olau Cliffs on the windward side of Oahu savagely tested our resolve and our stamina. The more cautious ones of our group drifted to the rear. The two narrow tunnels we had to run through at the top of the grade forced us against the walls whenever a car came through. Spotting our battery-powered lights, the few drivers on the road that Christmas morning slowed down to honk their car horns, roll down their windows, and cheer us on.

"I can't believe you talked us into doing this, Jo," Rory gasped. "Count me in for next year!"

"After this, we can spend the rest of the day lying around eating. What's better than that?" I panted. I always had my eye on the reward beyond the effort—it was the way I looked at everything in my life at that time.

We had been running for about eleven miles when Rox piped up from the back of the pack, "This Santa's elf is tired! When the truck comes back I'm quitting!" Her words came out between wheezes.

"No!" we all shouted. "You can't quit, it's only five more miles."

"Five more miles? I'll be dead by then! Who has an oxygen tank?"

"Here comes the truck!" Gail shouted as Rocky and Ian pulled up alongside us. I noticed bags of pork rinds and Funyuns on the front seat, evidence of why they were driving the truck and not running with us. Dan, the guy Rox was dating, kept pace with her and handed her a bottle of water. She sat on the sidewalk and stretched while we tried to convince her to continue.

"Come on, Rox, you can't quit. We'll slow the pace down," I said.

"Yeah, Rox," Rory said. "We all started it, so we all gotta finish it."

Rox wasn't buying any of it, but she sucked it up and kept moving.

The truck pulled away, and we started running again. I was glad to be rid of the smell of pork rinds. Our pace now slowed to an agonizing crawl, but it allowed us to laugh and talk. With sixteen miles behind us, Waterfront Park finally came into view.

Rocky and Ian were waiting for us. Whooping with joy as we jogged in, we felt like we deserved our own ticker tape parade. Instead, two sleepy security guards, counting on a quiet holiday, ignored our celebration.

"We did it!" I shrieked just as Rory poured a bottle of ice water over my head. After water fights, pictures, and videos, we climbed into the back of the truck for the drive back to Kailua. Parking the truck a few blocks from my house, we made a beeline for Kailua Beach where we jumped into the ocean fully clothed. This was the celebration of the life I lived daily—a spectacular day; one of many I took for granted.

In Hawaii, strangers can become friends quickly while friends become family. Good friends sometimes moved away, but I had Gail, Cindy, Rory, and Rox in my life for more than ten years. These guys were always ready for an adventure. Before I sold my house, Rory and Rox both rented rooms there. A weekly household tradition was our Sunday-morning mini triathlon. No matter how late our music gigs ended the night before, the three of us would hoof it to the beach at sunrise where we swam, ran, and rollerbladed for three hours or more. We were steel.

Loads of people think they want to live in Hawaii. Many come and fewer stay. It's a revolving door—a kaleidoscope of characters trying to find a way to live the dream. The cost of island life is so high that it is difficult for many people to make it work.

To maintain the quality of life I desired, I balanced three high-powered careers—professional musician, exercise therapist/ personal trainer, and radio personality. Each had an intensity that matched my athletic training, and each involved people. Always in the public eye, I was making a wonderful living in a gorgeous place doing exactly what I wanted to do.

I loved my life.

3

The Art of Confession

If we only have the will to walk, then God
is pleased with our stumbles.

—C. S. LEWIS

I was raised in a Catholic home. Throughout my life, I believed God was real. I never doubted He was the Creator of the universe. Although I believed Jesus was the Son of God, I had never been introduced to Him as my personal Savior. I only heard about the Holy Spirit when we recited the Profession of Faith each week at church.

My family attended Sunday Mass regularly until I turned thirteen, the year I began to question why I had to go to confession. Equally troubling to me were the assigned prayers I had to recite as penance for my infractions. I asked my parents why we had to sit in a confessional box to tell a priest our sins. I asked the same question of the nuns and brothers teaching us

11

catechism. I set about to get an answer from Sister Mary Agnes during preparation for my Catholic confirmation.

"Excuse me, Sister. Can I ask a question?"

Sister Mary Agnes peered at me above her half glasses while she used another bobby pin to secure Carolyn's confirmation headpiece. "If it is about the name you have been assigned for your confirmation—no."

I moved closer, hoping proximity would give me the answer I wanted.

"It isn't about that. I am wondering why I can't just tell God my sins and ask Him to forgive me, instead of going to the priest in the confessional every week."

Sister Agnes replied with finality: "Joanne, only those with perfect contrition may seek the forgiveness of God outside of the Sacrament of Confession. That is certainly not the case with you. The only way to have our grave sins forgiven is through the admission of sin to the priest. He will proclaim you free from sin and assign penance through our Lord Jesus Christ."

I sighed without remark. I'd heard this before, and I knew that my bullheadedness was about to get me into trouble.

As was traditional in my family, we attended midnight mass each Christmas Eve. We all endured the late-evening service in order to come home for soup and gain permission to open one gift. Church attendance was a form of bribery. My mom always insisted we had to get there at least two hours early to get a good spot.

One Christmas Eve we streamed out our front door at ten o'clock to secure six seats together at our church in southern Prince George's County, Maryland, a suburb of Washington DC. After surveying the growing sea of humanity, we found an almost-empty pew on the right side of the large cathedral-style church. After the crowd settled in, the service went along as usual until it was time for confession.

Along the sides of the church closest to the altar stood two red-draped confessional boxes flanking a center box in which the priest assigned to hear confessions sat. Inside the confessional and behind the closed curtain, the penitent would kneel. A small screen, about a foot in diameter, would slide open, and the priest sitting on the other side would wait to hear the prescribed words: "Bless me, Father, for I have sinned; it has been [the place and time frame] since my last confession."

The whole process made me twitch. I didn't have a problem confessing what I had done wrong. I simply couldn't remember the number of times I slugged my brother, sassed my mom, or talked mean about someone else. The nuns taught us that we needed to identify the number of times we did something wrong to be absolved of the sin of each incident. I racked my brain trying to remember the time, place, and frequency of my infractions. My armpits sweated, and my stomach hatched butterflies.

Why can't I just tell You, God? Why do I have to go into those creepy boxes?

My mom's whisper interrupted my inner dialogue. "The lines are really long, and our turn is coming up. Follow me down the center aisle, and we'll go to the confessional on the right."

"I'm going to go to the ones in the back. The lines look shorter," I whispered back.

She nodded. "Okay, meet us back here."

At that moment I knew I would need to confess what I was about to do. I ambled to the back of the church, and, bypassing the long line now almost circling the transept, I exited the building and skulked around the corner of the church complex in the bitter winter cold.

I'm sorry, God, but this whole thing makes no sense to me.

As I reentered the back door to return to my seat, I noticed my mom and siblings headed back to our pew. My mom knelt next to me on the kneeler pad in front of us and leaned over to whisper in my ear.

"The line must have been much shorter back there."

"Not really, it just moved really fast," I lied, while trying to avoid her eyes.

This was the beginning of my family's slide into spotty attendance. During the next six months, my mother grew weary of battling with me to go to church each Sunday. My father and siblings were happy to join my protests. Eventually we became a family of "Chreasters": Christmas and Easter attendees only. Finally, I was free of the creepy confessional.

Unfortunately, my idea to go directly to God with my requests for forgiveness faded right along with our church attendance. I began to see myself as the author of my own destiny. I knew God was there, but I pushed Him farther out of my world.

※

My family moved from the East Coast to Hawaii when I was sixteen. I began formal music training there. Former members of the Italian opera trained me in the art of singing known as bel canto. I had played piano and organ since elementary school and sang since almost my first breath. From the age of five, I knew I would be a professional musician. Later, I was certain it was God who had planted the idea in me at that young age.

"What do you want to be what you grow up, Squidly?" my father asked me when I was seven. Squidly was his favorite name for me.

"I'm going to be a singer. That's all I want to do."

"You need to figure out another plan, Joanne. You can't just sing and make a living," he said.

"Yeah? Just watch me, Dad."

Even as a small child, I would set my sight on a goal and there was little anyone could say or do to deter me.

I charged into the Hawaiian music scene like a big wave rider storming Waimea Bay. I was undaunted by the fact that I was a *haole* (Hawaiian for "white person"). In Hawaii, *haoles* don't just launch into the local music scene. For some reason, I was granted favor and at seventeen began performing in some of the most prestigious venues on the islands. I enjoyed great success as a soloist, songwriter, recording artist, and radio personality for twenty-two years. I had wanted the musician's life from the time I was five, and I was living my dream.

God was gracious and compassionate toward me. He allowed me to live out the desires of my heart, even though I had all but forgotten Him except in moments of great need. From my early days of catechism, I remembered that treating others as you want to be treated was important to God. I made every effort to live this way. When my friends needed help I opened my home, my heart, and my wallet. I experienced great joy at being able to reach out to others. But I still didn't know God personally.

At the same time my music career began, diet and exercise infiltrated my way of life. I became fascinated with the idea of reshaping the human body. In the years that followed, I pushed myself further to become certified by the American College of Sports Medicine as a personal trainer and exercise therapist. I took advanced certification programs in nutrition, obesity, and cardiac rehabilitation.

By day I trained a growing list of private therapy clients,

while running multiple high-end fitness and wellness centers. In addition I hosted radio shows, playing contemporary R&B music while providing music, culture, and trend commentary that aired in both Hawaii and Japan. My producers on Oahu loved when I was on the air. The switchboard lit up with 50 percent of the callers from Oahu Correctional Center. The joke around the station was that it didn't matter what music I played, the inmates just wanted to hear me talk because my voice was lower than most men's.

I lived out my music career at night. My workdays routinely extended over eighteen hours. I would crawl into bed just before 2:00 a.m., only to be awakened by my alarm at 4:00 to get ready to train by 5:00. I thought I had it all—except enough sleep. While it was exhilarating to do the things I was passionate about, I discovered a candle cannot burn at both ends forever.

4

Highway Jesus

Jesus didn't say, "Blessed are those who care for the poor." He said, "Blessed are we where we are poor, where we are broken." It is there that God loves us deeply and pulls us into deeper communion with himself.

—HENRY NOUWEN

Years evaporated like summer rain on steaming blacktop and along with them my marriage of nine years. When I was twenty-four, I married a nice guy with addictive behaviors. When I married him, I was naïve, headstrong, and convinced that—with enough personal resolve and self-discipline—most problems could be overcome. I viewed his inability to quit drugs and alcohol as lack of will, weak character, and, on certain occasions, a personal offense—it was something I thought he did on purpose to hurt me.

Disappointed by his failure to free himself from addiction, I emotionally divorced myself from him long before I filed the legal paperwork. I no longer wanted to be married. Although divorce had been my idea, I was emotionally devastated by the reality of it. Marriage was supposed to be forever, and I had failed. I faced this hurdle with characteristic resolve, forcing myself to focus on my careers and forging ahead.

My divorce settlement and the Hawaii real estate crash of the '90s left me penniless and mired in a sea of debt. Although I kept the house, my savings disappeared when I handed over my ex-husband's share of the equity. In the end I was forced to sell my beautiful house at an enormous loss. My heart continued to break as, unable to find a rental property that allowed large dogs, I lost my beloved golden retrievers as well.

My divorce then took a physical toll on me. Plagued by anxiety, I dropped fifteen pounds of muscle almost overnight. My feelings of guilt for leaving my marriage choked out sleep. I took to the streets Rollerblading or running—even at 2:00 a.m.— ten to fifteen miles at a time to silence the voice of shame that accompanied my thoughts. My friends stood by me through it all, bringing me chicken soup and serving up wisdom by the ladleful.

In the middle of this, my doctors issued a frightening mandate: complete voice rest for thirty days because of a cyst that had formed on my vocal cords. My careers in music, radio, and personal training all came to a halt. I canceled music performances, radio shows, and physical training appointments. I was left with virtually no income stream. In a few months, the financial stability I had worked so hard for slipped away. I simply could not catch up financially by working harder—there were not enough hours in the day.

To avoid surgery, my vocal cords could not be constricted in any way. Since laughter tightened my throat, and because my friends always made me laugh, I had no visitors.

The isolation was torturous, but in my solitude, I began to think about God. I wrestled with Him: *What did I do to deserve this? I'm a good person, right? I try to do good things for people, don't I? There are so many people doing terrible things around me, and they don't have these problems. This isn't fair!*

I felt persecuted, abandoned, and, for the first time in my life, unable to see my way through my problems. I tried meditation—it didn't work. I tried going back to the Catholic Church, sitting inconspicuously on the rear pew during mass—it didn't work.

Still searching, I tried another Christian church. Taking a Bible from the seatback pocket, I began to read from the beginning. The Old Testament lost me somewhere in the book of Numbers—I didn't know who all these people were or who begat whom. Who cared, anyway? Growing impatient, I turned toward the back of the book to the New Testament. I read it, but I struggled with its meaning.

My parents always taught me to work hard, save my money, be kind to everyone, and help whenever I could. This was the recipe for personal success. Hadn't I done all of that? Despite my best efforts, however, my self-made life had been completely dismantled in a year.

I had been resolute in my belief that I had control over every aspect of my life. I had created my success by sheer grit, determination, discipline, and unquenchable optimism. I didn't believe God deserved the credit for any of my accomplishments. I had done all the things I thought would bring a full, happy, and successful life. Where did I go wrong?

Although voice rest forced me to take a leave of absence from my fitness business, I made an exception for one of my personal training clients who was wheelchair bound. A client for ten years, she had no intention of missing her home therapy sessions while I was on voice rest. Driving away from her house in the hills above Honolulu after her therapy session one afternoon, I began to sob hysterically. I was worried, alone, sick, silent, and broke for the first time in my life.

The winding, narrow road down the steep mountainside was no place for my blubbering. A tidal wave of hopelessness crashed over me with such force that I nearly lost my grip on the wheel. I tried to wipe my tear-filled eyes to see where I was driving when the skies unleashed a winter deluge. I really didn't care anymore. Everything was out of control. I might as well lose control of the car too.

As I drove, my thoughts raced to the vial of sleeping pills I had back at the house. My doctor had prescribed them for the sleepless nights brought on by my divorce. The full bottle called to me now. Going to sleep forever sounded inviting—a way out of the hopelessness facing me.

I jerked myself back from my depressive thoughts to focus on the wet, curvy road. The storm continued as I hurled down the Honolulu freeway and moved into the middle lane. In a raspy, bruised voice, I cried out to God: "What did I do to deserve this? I'm a good person! Why do You hate me? Haven't I lost enough? Come on! My health too? You can't possibly be real! If You were real, You'd show me! You'd show me right now!"

Just then, when the last phrase left my lips, a white Volkswagen van cut me off. As it cleared my front fender, I looked at the license plate: DEUT 6:5.

I was shaken out of my spiraling thoughts and looked again. *Wait a minute. That looks like some sort of Bible verse.* My mind raced as I remembered, just weeks before, seeing something in the Bible that looked like this. Mystified by the encounter and terrified about what I might discover, I resolved to look up the verse when I got home. Was this some sort of answer from God? Was He really there? Was He really listening to my ranting?

Still shaking, I pulled into my driveway at 2:20 in the afternoon. As I entered my little rental house, my thoughts returned to the sleeping pills.

The Bible I had been reading lay on the coffee table where I had left it the night before. I took the bottle from the medicine cabinet and placed it next to the Bible. I sat down in the chair next to the open window across the room. For hours I sat and stared at the Bible and the bottle of pills.

I contemplated my freeway encounter. I pored over the elements of my life that had me cornered now. I had a choice to make. I could open the Bible and find out if the freeway incident had been nothing but coincidence—or maybe God did drive a Volkswagen van—or I could swallow the sleeping pills and be done with this living nightmare. The battle in my mind raged on until dusk. *What if the God of the universe is real?*

After hours of contemplation, I finally concluded that if Deut. 6:5 turned out to be nothing, I would take the sleeping pills. I now had a plan. I assumed control again.

I got up from my chair and grabbed the Bible. I sat on the couch and turned to the table of contents. I scanned to see if DEUT resembled anything there. It did—the book of Deuteronomy. I discovered that the number 6 was the chapter of the book, and the number 5 was the verse in that chapter. I took a deep breath and read, "Love the LORD your God with all your heart, all your soul, and all your strength" (NIV).

I certainly hadn't been doing that. Until that moment I had believed that I held all the cards. It never occurred to me that something or someone else had control over my destiny. I set my own goals, created my own opportunities, and designed my own destiny. My success was due to my strengths, my talents, and my determination. This strategy had served me well until my house of cards came crashing down.

Deuteronomy 6:5 continued. Loving the Lord with all my heart, soul, and strength should be on my heart and taught to my children. I must fear the Lord, serve Him, and do what is right in His eyes. The verses explained that things would go well with me if I abided in this way. It was a promise from God. I couldn't breathe as the crushing weight of truth pressed upon my heart. God might really be the one in charge after all.

Overwhelmed, I knelt on the floor. Fresh tears dropped on the pages of the Bible, matching the raindrops against the window. The words I read took on new meaning as I reviewed my life decisions and my current situation. Stunned, I knew that the freeway incident could not be a coincidence.

I asked God to take charge of my life. I surrendered my will and prayed for forgiveness. Peace overcame me, replacing the storm of chaos that had overwhelmed me earlier. I knew now I was not alone. Whatever situations I faced, I knew God was bigger. Without a doubt, I knew that God existed. I knew He alone had extended His grace and mercy to allow me to do what I had wanted all these years. It was now time to do what He wanted me to do.

I prayed and read God's written words through the night. The urge to end my life subsided, replaced by repose and trust as I felt God at work in me. When I let go of control of my life and accepted His divine help, I felt I could take a full, deep breath for the first time in nearly a year. He had a plan.

My freeway encounter with God changed my life. I now

knew a God who cared. I vowed to never lose hope despite my circumstances. My sister Patty describes this transformation as optimism to the tenth power. I call it optimism by the only power—Jesus.

5

What Love Does

You can give without loving.
But you cannot love without giving.
—AMY CARMICHAEL, MISSIONARY AND
FOUNDER OF AN ORPHANAGE IN INDIA

After my encounter with Jesus on the freeway and after my divorce was finalized, I began dating Mike Moody—the sweetest man I have ever known. Life brightened for me in the glow of his keen sense of humor, and his brown eyes held a deep sincerity that I loved. We met when he was in Honolulu on a short-term work assignment, but when that was finished, he moved back to his home in the San Francisco area.

In time my voice returned, but new, chronic health issues plagued me. I continued to battle hoarseness, as well as ongoing pneumonia, bronchitis, and stomach issues. I had regained some of the weight I had lost during my divorce, but now it was dropping again—along with my hair. Unexplained fatigue and constant joint pain were added to my growing list of maladies.

A battery of diagnostic tests followed. The doctors concluded my symptoms were due to fibromyalgia, thyroid malfunction, and irritable bowel syndrome. Although they gave me meds, nothing relieved my symptoms.

I didn't know my own body anymore. I could no longer depend on the physical strength and stamina I had developed through twenty years of rigorous training. Exercise was always my compass. Now, without it, I had no gauge to tell me how much strength I had to accomplish all the things I had to do throughout the day.

I not only had to battle for my health, but I had to deal with the financial repercussions of a reduced work schedule and debt from the short sale of my house. I prayed, "God, I know You are real. Can You see me? Please, I need Your help. I'm so tired."

When Mike learned of my failing health and mounting debt, he decided to return to Honolulu to be with me, accepting another short-term assignment in the information technology field. I wrestled with my reaction to his decision. Deep down, I felt like a failure—I didn't know how to receive assistance, and I didn't want to burden Mike with my shortcomings. I was glad he wanted to come, but there was no one who could bail me out of the mess, no one but me.

My resolve to remain independent softened through the laughter Mike ushered into our conversations. His willingness to stand beside me felt like a new pair of shoes—uncomfortable at first, but now I never wanted to take them off.

My circumstances became troubling to others, and news of it began to spread. Two of my clients, who were also dear friends of fifteen years, telephoned my mother in Florida to let her know how concerned they were about me. They conspired with my parents and other incredible family and friends to give me a birthday present that would change my life.

Mike, in on the surprise, brought me my mail one afternoon as I was lying in bed resting. A manila envelope from the bank lay on the top of weekly circulars and bills. Uneasy about the possibility of new problems, I opened the envelope. It contained a single piece of paper—the loan document from the short sale of my house—marked "Paid in Full." My debt had been settled, and I owed no more money! I read and reread the words. I could not understand how any of this could have taken place. Then Mike spoke up.

"This is the best birthday present we could think of, honey. Everyone wants you to be well."

I sobbed with the revelation that I was free—out from under seemingly insurmountable debt. I thanked God, who I suspected might have had something to do with it.

Mike and I attended a nondenominational church on Sundays. When my health permitted, I sometimes played keyboards and sang on the worship team. I was new to this church culture that was so different from my Catholic background. The bonds of my newfound faith were so tenuous and my wounds so fresh that when the senior pastor was asked to step down because of mental health issues, I wanted to bolt. I reasoned that I didn't need any more stress in my life than I already had.

On my last Sunday there, I listened to two visiting pastors from Torrance, California, speak at both the morning and evening services. They began by speaking about love—God is love, for love, about love; we were created by love.

This was not a new message for me—I had learned about God's love in my new church home—but their words sounded fresh, and I was intrigued. They spoke of how extravagantly our heavenly Father loves us—how He sees us as perfect and sinless through the sacrifice of Jesus. They talked about the "Father heart" of God. What a far cry from the guilt, shame, and fear I had known in my earlier religious experiences. This was more profound than any teaching I had ever heard.

When the evening service ended, as I got up to leave, both pastors approached me. They told me God had chosen me to do great things for Him in the realms of leadership, music, and writing. They told me it was not a mistake I was there. New to all of this, I listened to their encouragement and graciously thanked them. I headed out before they could see how deeply the conversation moved me.

Their words stayed with me. I mulled over their message of love for weeks. As I struggled to understand the Father's heart of love for me, I was drawn to God's Word as never before.

I discovered John 3:17–18: "For God did not send the Son into the world to judge the world, but that the world might be saved through Him. He who believes in Him is not judged . . ." Revelation flooded me as I realized that I could never earn more of His love than I already had. He didn't need me to be perfect or to perform for Him in order for me to be blessed by Him. He simply loves me as I am.

What an amazing truth. Although I didn't fully receive it then, it made sense to me. With fresh perspective, I began to assess my life and all that I had been living for.

The Torrance pastors returned several times to the church. As a result, Mike and I continued to attend there for a few more months. Each time they spoke we heard more about the love of God. It was like drinking cold water after living in the desert for thirty years. I couldn't get enough. Mike had been a Christian growing up, although he had fallen away in college. One night, the younger of the two pastors prophesied that Mike had a gift for teaching God's Word. After praying, the pastor gave Mike his Bible.

"With what God has planned for you, Mike, you'll need this more than I will."

That moment was a powerful display of God's love for Mike. I was in awe of the Lord and His timing. Shouts of praise and joy rang out from our friends as Mike rededicated his life to Christ.

The Torrance pastors invited me to a women's retreat at their church in California. I didn't have any extra money, and after researching the price of airfares, I declined the invitation. The financial realities of travel did not change my desire to go, so I made a beginner's attempt to give the matter to God in prayer, asking Him to provide a way for me if He wanted me to go. Before the end of the week, my feeble prayer had been answered when I received two unexpected checks in the mail: one from my insurance company and the other from my former bank. *Seriously!* I thought. *What insurance company or bank ever gives away money?*

As I opened the envelope from my bank, I found that the check inside was made out to me for the exact amount of the airfare I had researched days before. *You have my attention, God. I don't understand why You do these things for me, but thank You.* I opened the second envelope, which contained a check in an amount that would cover my lost wages for the time I would be gone. *Are you kidding me, God?* Joy, pure joy, broke out all over my face as I skipped up to my front door.

≫✦≪

When I arrived at the retreat, I was exhausted. I had no energy for small talk. *God, I know You brought me here, but I am tired and I don't want to make new friends I will never see again.* I determined the best strategy was to sit by myself in the back of the room.

At the first large-group gathering of the evening, my strategy failed when the speaker pointed to me from the front of the conference room and called me to come forward. My stomach lurched and my face turned crimson. So much for hiding in the back of the room filled with two hundred women.

As I reached the front of the room, the speaker said, "You've traveled the farthest distance of anyone here. You've had great struggles, but God is for you. You live in the islands and you sing. Yes, you sing! You are highly esteemed by God, and He has great plans for you. You will sing, but you will sing prophetically. You will sing for Him. Your life will be to heal the sick, cast out demons, and raise the dead!"

As she was speaking, my body bent forward on its own volition and began shaking like crazy under the power of God. She raised her hand in front of my forehead, not touching it, and I began to fall backward. I felt someone behind me catch me and ease me to the floor. On the way down, my brain screamed, *This is crazy. What are you doing? Get hold of yourself!*

The shaking continued, but the chatter in my mind ceased when the full magnitude of the presence of God came over me. His presence was so enormous that everything else faded away, and I felt as tiny as a speck of dust. I had never experienced His presence in this manner. In my mind, I heard Him softly whisper things that only I could hear. Everything He said confirmed the speaker's words. He told me not to fear, to let go of control, and to allow Him to lead and bless me. I was shaking too uncontrollably to respond verbally, but in my heart I answered, *Yes, Lord. Whatever You want.*

That touch from God destroyed my plan for anonymity at the conference—I could no longer remain "invisible" to the women around me.

"You are new to all of this, huh?" asked Michelle. I had watched her dance around during worship and admired her freedom to move in adoration of God.

"I have no idea what's going on," I replied and then laughed.

"You should come up front and dance with us. It's awesome."

"Umm. I'll come up closer to the front to sit but I'll leave the dancing to you guys," I said.

"Okay, but it's just the first night. You might change your mind. I have a feeling we're going to be good friends."

I know in God's world we are all brothers and sisters, but that weekend I met lifelong friends all because God's love is spread by contact with human beings. Incredible.

At the end of the retreat, the husband of one of the attendees approached me in the parking lot. "I don't want to come across as a weirdo or anything, but I saw you in a dream last night. You live in Hawaii, but God is going to bring you to this area. He's going to do this to bless you."

I stared at him, trying to process what he was saying. I had never seen this man before. I had met his wife only briefly at the retreat, and she was still inside the conference center. He smiled as he went in to find her.

What are You doing now, God?

⋇

I was deeply affected by what I had experienced at the women's conference, and I knew I had to make some changes in my life. Mike and I began to talk about the future. His new job in

Hawaii was contractual and would eventually end. Although I had gotten my careers back on track, my health was another matter. It was clear that my body needed more than just a day off here and there to fully recover.

More than once Mike told me, "I just want to give you a rest, Jo. Let's get married and move to California. You can stop working for a while, and I can take care of you." I was still uncomfortable with the idea of being taken care of, but my overachieving and independent self was completely and utterly exhausted. After many months of prayer, I accepted Mike's offer and made the decision to walk away from my old life.

Mike was offered a permanent job in Compton, California. A few weeks after he received the offer, we found out the job was located in Torrance. His new office was a mile and a half from the Torrance church we had grown to love. I don't know why I was surprised. Still new to the power and workings of God, I smiled a lot and shook my head in wonder and disbelief. Mike and I saw God move in so many ways, we couldn't help but laugh about it. Our relocation to Torrance was like a family homecoming as our new Christian friends and pastors embraced and discipled us.

Two weeks after our arrival in Torrance, we were married on a hilltop in Palos Verdes, overlooking the ocean. Even given the short notice, our family members came to stand with us, flanked by seventy-five of our new church friends.

Our new friends bestowed such generosity on us we were dumbfounded. The kindness of God was evident in every detail—from the gorgeous raw-silk wedding dress Trista gave me to the grass Todd mowed on the ceremony hilltop. Mike and I were secure in our decision and stood hand in hand while the rainy skies over the California coast parted for the first time in two weeks just as we said, "I do."

Thank You, God. Here is where I belong.

I finally experienced rest for the first time in my adult life.

⁂

A few months after our wedding, I attended another women's retreat sponsored by our Torrance church, this time in Orange County. A young woman I knew came up to me and said, "I was just praying back there, and I'm probably nuts telling you this, but I feel like God wants me to give you a message. The message is Deuteronomy 6:5. Does that mean anything to you?"

Tears ran down my face. All I could do was nod. She could not have known it was the verse God had used to save my life. He was speaking to me loud and clear again. When I let her know the magnitude of the word she had delivered to me, she sobbed too.

"That's the first time I've ever heard God," she said.

6

The Delivery

"Fo' Gawd, Miss Scarlett! We's got ter have a doctah. Ah-Ah-Miss Scarlett, Ah doan know nuthin' 'bout bringin' babies."

—PRISSY, FROM *GONE WITH THE WIND*
BY MARGARET MITCHELL

Just a little more time," the obstetric nurse said as she darted from the room.

The Nubain took effect, and I started to retch. Mike pushed the call button for the nurse to come, but it was an hour before she returned to hand him a bedpan.

"Isn't there something else you could give her?" Mike asked as I vomited into the pan.

"With her allergies, Nubain really is the best choice."

The drug helped decrease the pain a bit, but the violent retching persisted. Hours passed as I prayed for my cervix to dilate, but there was no change. Nurses bustled in and out of my room, administering more Nubain as the earlier doses wore off. Throughout the night, Mike asked the nurses again and again to page Dr. Fletcher, but the calls to the doctor went unanswered. Between heaving and battling exhaustion, I tried to practice the Bradley breathing and counting methods that Mike and I had learned. That long night eventually became the next day.

"You aren't helping me, Mike!" I wailed.

"Honey, I'm counting like we practiced. Your contractions aren't following any pattern. I don't know what else to do."

They hadn't told us what to do in the birthing class if contractions weren't normal. Tears were my only response.

Late in the morning, my natural childbirth coach turned up and told a beleaguered Mike and the nurses that she thought a Caesarean should be done. Since I knew she was a staunch proponent of natural birth, it alarmed me that even she had given up hope that I could deliver this baby naturally. After she shared her concerns, she and a nurse began to pray over me. As they laid hands on my body, I heard them pray for some relief from my pain while I silently begged God not to let anything happen to my baby.

Dr. Fletcher breezed into the room late that afternoon. We had not talked to her since I first came to the hospital. That she had not answered the nurse's previous calls or sent word to me caused me to be filled with anxiety. *God, please help. She's cruel and indifferent, and I am trapped.*

"Joanne, I will be handling your delivery. We're going to give you Pitocin to speed up your labor, and you'll be delivering in no time. Everything looks fine." Like a cold north wind, she whirled around and left the room.

The Pitocin IV was placed in my arm, but hours passed with no change. The contractions that had begun early Sunday morning moved into midday Tuesday; I had been in labor for more than two-and-a-half days. A monitor beeped, and the IV pinched, as another wave of nausea made me retch for what seemed like the thousandth time.

Although the staff tried to make me as comfortable as possible, Mike and I sensed a growing concern from the nurses, who kept scurrying in and out of the room. I was crying and so weak from the heaving and the pain that I was barely able to maintain consciousness. Mike wasn't doing much better. Time became a barometer of my mounting torment as Tuesday evening crept in. I didn't want to look at a clock anymore. No one was helping me.

Night became day once more, but the light in my heart had dulled to barely a flicker. A nurse told us that I would not be given epidural pain relief until my cervix was dilated to three centimeters. I was going mad trying to find a place for my brain to focus on something that did not include pain.

Where are you, God? What is going on? Silence. Then a sudden remembrance of His Word flashed into my mind. "Where does my help come from? My help comes from the LORD, the Maker of heaven and earth" (Psalm 121:1–2 NIV).

Around 6:00 p.m., my cervix finally dilated a few centimeters. That progress brought Dr. Fletcher, with her usual cold-front flair.

"Okay, Joanne. I'm going to break your water and speed things up."

I clenched my teeth, while fighting the urge to vomit. "Why didn't you do that earlier if it is supposed to speed things up? Why did you leave me here to suffer this long without any progress?"

She avoided both my gaze and my question.

"We need to get a monitor on your baby's head, and we have

to break your water to do it. It increases your risk of infection, so the nurse will watch for that," she said.

As she examined me, I felt such a sharp pain—like something wasn't right in there. I tried to explain the pain, but she patted my arm like I was a five-year-old and clucked for me not to worry. Before leaving, she finally ordered the epidural.

"Make them take the baby out," I cried to Mike, after she left. "I can't handle this anymore."

I was sobbing, near hysterics.

Mike was exhausted and teary-eyed. "Please, can't you do something for my wife? Can't you make the doctor order a C-section?" he asked a nurse.

"Mr. Moody, we are all in agreement this has gone on too long, but we're powerless here. We can't even give an aspirin without a doctor's order. This doctor makes her own decisions, and she doesn't welcome advice from us," she replied.

I am undone, God. I am left to the mercy of a cruel and unfeeling woman. Why is this happening to me?

If God responded to my cries, I was too far gone to notice. It was 10:50 p.m.

Dehydrated, spent, and overwhelmed by agony, I intermittently blacked out. A compassionate, bleary-eyed nurse told us I had finally dilated to nine centimeters and that I could start pushing soon. Was she serious? I didn't have enough strength left to push a peanut through the birth canal, let alone a baby.

The nurse checked the baby's status before coaching me to push. "The baby's heart rate is dropping!"

"What's happening to my baby?" I yowled as I came to after a blackout. Nurses were running in and speaking in frantic whispers. One leaned over me.

"Don't worry, help's coming."

Panic and confusion erupted as the on-call obstetrician was paged. I was hurriedly prepped for an emergency C-section. They wheeled me into the operating room, and an already masked female doctor walked over to me.

"Don't worry. Your baby will be fine. We have the neonatal specialist on the way, and he will pull your baby out to make sure he's okay after I make the initial incision. You will feel some tugging even though you are numb from the waist down. Do you wear a bikini?"

"What? Yeah, but—" The anesthesia mask covered my mouth before I could finish. I heard heels clicking and watched Dr. Fletcher walk in. I heard her say she would be assisting. I was too weak to protest.

After being stranded in the birth canal for days, our son, Kian, arrived at 11:32 p.m. Other than suffering from jaundice, he was perfect.

We didn't see Dr. Fletcher again for two days, not until she came into my room to perform Kian's circumcision. There was no mention of my traumatic delivery. The nurse followed with Kian.

"This will only take a minute."

In a few seconds, and after one loud cry from Kian, it was done. The doctor pulled off her latex gloves and headed out the door. Mike held Kian, and we stared at each other in disbelief. We never saw her again.

My own obstetrician, Dr. Smith, came to see me in the hospital two days later. He authorized Motrin and Vicodin for the duration of the healing from my C-section. His incredibly kind and gentle nature made all his patients adore him.

"This should never have happened, Joanne. I'm so sorry," he said, as he pulled up a chair next to my hospital bed. I saw the fatigue in his eyes as he told me about the recent death of his father. "Yours is the only birth I missed, and I promised you I would be here."

My eyes filled with tears.

"If we had ordered an ultrasound, we could have seen that Kian's head was too large to fit through your pelvic canal. If you and Mike decide to have another child, I will schedule a C-section in advance."

"Dr. Smith, I really appreciate you explaining this to us, but if I ever think about having another baby, I'll buy a hamster."

Although Dr. Smith never mentioned Dr. Fletcher by name, Mike and I certainly did after he left the room.

"I think he just apologized for Dr. Fletcher's screw-up, don't you?" Mike asked.

"Maybe. I can't think about it anymore. I just want to focus on Kian being born healthy. We could be sitting here without him, you know."

I offered a prayer of thanks to God for the little bundle in my arms and tried to push away the horror of what I had just endured for ninety-one hours.

7

Life Is Different Now

Making the decision to have a child—it's momentous.
It is to decide forever to have your heart go
walking around outside your body.

—ELIZABETH STONE, AUTHOR OF *A BOY I ONCE KNEW*

I spent most of the following weeks flat on my back as my mom, Mike's parents, and a huge assortment of faithful friends took turns caring for us. Although being a new mom was exhilarating, my recovery was slow, and my pelvic area still burned with pain. Kian was my first child, so I assumed the pain was part of the normal recovery process and would fade as my C-section healed. Each day I made repeated efforts to believe that I felt normal—or as normal as any woman can feel when coping with a new baby.

I was in love with Kian and our new little family, and I held my son in my arms as I lay in bed. How many times a day can you kiss your baby? I stared at his perfect little face and thanked God he was born without any casualties from his traumatic birth. My mom had often told me that her greatest achievement and God's most precious gift to her was her children. I used to think it odd that she didn't aspire to be something other than a wife and mother.

I smiled as I now realized how she felt. Before Kian, I thought my greatest achievements were the career goals I had attained. Now, with Kian in my life, I saw that it was like comparing pyrite to gold. Being in relationship with God, sharing my life with a devoted man of God, and raising this little boy made my heart overflow with gratitude.

Less than two weeks after Kian's birth, I made a follow-up appointment with Dr. Smith. After such a chaotic beginning, I had settled into a routine of sorts, although the pain in my pelvic area had gotten worse. I could tolerate mornings, but by mid-afternoon the pain forced me to lie down. I told Dr. Smith that the searing pain and agonizing pressure in my groin area felt like my uterus was about to fall out. Suspecting a urinary infection, he ordered lab tests. He called the next day to tell me the test had come back negative.

"There's no point in putting you on antibiotics, Joanne," Dr. Smith said. "I think we just need to manage the pain. I'll give you one more refill of Vicodin, but after that you'll have to take Motrin if you're still uncomfortable. Vicodin has too many side effects and is too addicting to take it for any longer than that."

I left the office assuring myself everything would be fine. For the next month, I survived on a combination of Vicodin and Motrin, yet I felt far from fine. When the month ended and I had taken my last Vicodin, I could not sit or stand for more than a few minutes without my lower abdomen and pelvis burning with pain. Further testing revealed the presence of cysts and endometriosis, so the first of many surgeries was performed in May 1999, just four months after Kian was born.

The surgery completely debilitated me. Pain, like gasoline on a fire, roared through my pelvis day and night; increasing as the months wore on. Since I could no longer obtain narcotic medication from my doctor, a friend in our church who was dying of brain cancer brought me his Vicodin. Peter had less than six months to live. He and his wife lived across the street from us. He cried when he handed me an envelope with pain pills.

"I can't bear to watch you suffer, Joanne. I have permanent refills and I'll give you whatever you need to help you function. This is not right that your doctor isn't helping you."

Mike, Peter, Peter's wife, and I all hugged and cried. I was so grateful to him and to God for giving me something to take the edge off my pain.

≫≪

In early 2000, Mike was offered a position with his company in the Bay Area. Mike wanted to live where he grew up and could transfer easily, so we were sure the Lord had opened the door for us to relocate. Our family and friends packed us up, and we left Southern California to move in with my supportive in-laws. Mike worked like crazy while my in-laws kept Kian entertained.

My new HMO physician, believing endometriosis was the culprit, insisted that hormone reduction therapy was the answer. He put me through eight weeks of hormone-reduction injections with Lupron, which only increased the pain. My initial hope of a cure was dashed when I realized my condition was getting worse. Sitting or standing for more than a few minutes now caused me to buckle under the pain. Unable to treat my symptoms, the doctor insinuated the cause of my pain might be in my head. I was being set adrift in the medical-care maze. I determined the acronym HMO stood for Horrific Medical Opinion.

I finally found an internist willing to prescribe painkillers, but my vague diagnosis and recent Vicodin use deterred him from writing prescriptions for more than a few weeks. At an impasse, I prayed for medical help to arrive before the pain pills ran out.

During the next few weeks, I found a practice in the San Francisco area specializing in women's health and pelvic pain. I was optimistic that this was the breakthrough I was looking for. I called to make some preliminary inquiries, only to find they were not in our insurance network and the cost of treatment was out of the question for us. Still hanging on to the phone in my in-laws' kitchen, I sank to the floor in a flood of tears and frustration as I realized that the help I desperately needed was just out of reach. Another door slammed in my face.

My mom called the house later in the day and spoke to Roberta, my mom-in-law. I was in bed in their guest room when she brought me the phone.

"It's your mom, Jo. She's really worried and wants to know what happened. I told her about the practice not being in your insurance network," Roberta said as she handed me the phone. I could see the worry in her eyes.

I curled into a ball of convulsive sobs when I heard my mom's voice.

"Honey, we are not going to let you suffer. Make an appointment with this group. I'll catch a flight out. Don't worry about the money. I have a CD I can cash in, and I know Don will help."

Don was my mom's kind, generous, and loving boyfriend.

"I'll call your dad and your siblings too. Please, don't worry. We're here for you."

I was crying so hard I could barely answer—overwhelmed with gratitude, pain, and frustration with the powerlessness of my situation.

With the financial help from my family, I could be treated by the specialists at the clinic. More diagnostic tests rendered other theories and courses of treatment. During the next three years under their care, to alleviate my symptoms, I had five more surgeries, including a hysterectomy. What was going on here? Why was God allowing this to happen to me?

As I was prepped for each new surgery, the surgeon would assure me that this procedure was the one that would work. Yet each one failed. Between surgeries, I was using the strongest opiate pain medications on the market and suffering more than I thought a human being could. Every three-and-a-half hours, around the clock, I would take another round of opiates. This would buy me an hour of moderately dulled pain. It was in that brief span of time that I dared to take a deep breath. Chest breathing was the norm for me as it caused the least disturbance to my abdomen. I never needed to wear a watch. I could tell the time of day by my pain levels.

※

I couldn't carry my son for most of his young life. When my toddler reached up to me with his little arms, I had to kneel and pull him toward me instead. His words, "Mama, up!" filled my eyes with tears. To really hold him, I had to be lying down or completely reclined. I couldn't wait to be able to scoop him up off the floor and spin him around. Each of the failed surgeries reinforced what I could not do for my child and served as a reminder of the loss of physical intimacy in my marriage. My husband pressed on, but he suffered greatly.

I tried my best to look to Jesus and rest in Him—at times I could feel Him right beside me, and it was then that peace would wash over me. Invariably, however, the pain would overtake me and reduce me to tears. My emotions were raw, and my faith was on a roller-coaster ride. I knew God loved me. I knew He was there. I believed His Word and encountered the Holy Spirit, but I wondered how far my deep well of resiliency and faith could go before I ended my own life or had a nervous breakdown.

My faith was anchored in God, but the reality of my circumstances caused me to wonder about His nature. Was God allowing my suffering because He couldn't trust me to be compliant without it? My distorted belief was steeped in guilt from my Catholic upbringing and the perception that I would never measure up to what God expected of me. I carried my sin with me like a brick-filled suitcase. My dependency on others left me loading more bricks into my already bursting bag.

I was a giver, not a receiver. Being forced to receive for so long compelled me to ruminate on my own unworthiness. How would I ever repay what others had sacrificed for me? I often awoke in the deep of night with the realization of how much I owed everyone. The weight I felt in those moments often left me breathless. *God, why isn't this nightmare ending?* In the deepest hidden part of me, I began to feel persecuted by God, despite my love and fear of Him.

I still didn't understand the fullness of Jesus' love.

8

Dr. West and the Insurance Mess

The good physician treats the disease; the great physician treats the patient who has the disease.

—William Osler, cofounder of
Johns Hopkins Hospital

M ike stayed in the waiting room as I went into Dr. West's office in San Francisco for my consultation. I had been referred to Dr. West after the other clinic ran out of treatment options—every surgery, nerve block, and hormone treatment had failed. The nurse told me to make myself comfortable, motioning to a hard, wooden chair with a small cushion. I shook my head and squatted shakily against the wall instead.

"If I could cut myself off at the waist, I'd be comfortable," I told her.

"I've been with Dr. West for seventeen years, and I never get used to the suffering all of you are going through. You're in a good place, Joanne. He really knows what he's talking about."

I prayed she was right, as I tried to stuff down my cynicism.

Dr. West entered the room as his nurse left. He had a slight build, graying hair, a very kind face, and, as I was soon to learn, a quick wit. He shared a letter with me that had been written to him from the previous surgeon concerning my symptoms and surgeries.

"I'm sorry you weren't referred to me before these surgeries, Joanne. When that clinic sends patients to me, it's because they can't figure out what's causing the pain. Unfortunately, this means they've already operated on the patient, several times in your case. Almost always, the pain is never from endometriosis but from a condition of the muscles and connective tissue of the pelvic floor. The surgeries just exacerbate the condition. We'll know more after I examine you today, but the symptoms you are describing are likely to be caused by pelvic floor dysfunction or, possibly, pudendal nerve entrapment."

He escorted me to an exam room and left me to get undressed. A few minutes later he knocked on the door.

"Yep, I'm still here," I said.

"Well, by the looks of you, I didn't think you'd be running out the door," he said.

The exam and the sixteen trigger-point injection sites of steroids and local anesthetizing agents that followed were excruciating. By the time the exam was completed, I was shaking so badly that the nurse had to help me stand. Even though she steadied me, I hung on to the walls to get down the hallway. Between the pain and the two ice bags stuffed into the crotch area of my baggy overalls, it took me ten minutes to make it to the checkout desk. Mike stood up to greet me when I came around the corner, and I saw the worry in his eyes.

"You okay, honey?" he whispered.

I managed a weak nod. I couldn't speak for fear of having a total meltdown in the waiting room. Mike held me up as we headed out of the office to the parking garage. As he helped me lie down on the back seat of the car and shut the car door, I burst into tears—tears of pain and shock and hopelessness. I couldn't talk about the horror of the exam, the treatment, or Dr. West's diagnosis until the next day. Mike and I were both numb.

Dr. West's examination confirmed that I was suffering from pelvic floor dysfunction. The diagnosis of pudendal nerve entrapment could only be confirmed with a nerve latency test, which, due to the amount of pain I was experiencing, would be done when he was sure all other treatment modalities proved futile. As Dr. West had suspected, all the surgeries I had undergone to date had only exacerbated my condition.

Following my appointment with Dr. West, I began doing online research to understand my diagnosis—there was no cure, only treatments that promised mixed results. In some cases, symptoms were reduced with the treatment of trigger points and physical therapy. Where treatment was effective, it could take months before any improvement was experienced.

I read about patients returning to work and participating in life—always careful about posture and movement, but living life again. Among the mixed reviews, I saw a glimmer of hope—even the possibility of slight improvement was better than nothing.

⋇

As I moved ahead with treatment, I did not experience any significant or lasting relief. Mike supported me throughout, doing anything he could to help. He held me when I cried, brought me ice or heated flax bags, took care of Kian, and tucked me into bed every night.

We had lived with his parents for three months by now and knew we couldn't live with them forever. It was time to find our own home. As much as Mike wanted to raise Kian in his boyhood town, we faced the reality that we could not afford a home there. Mike discussed location options with his employer, and a transfer to the Sacramento area in Northern California was soon in the works. We purchased a small home in the suburbs of Sacramento and, with the help of our families, relocated to the fast-growing community of Rocklin.

Although our new home was a blessing, the two-hour drives to San Francisco for my weekly or biweekly medical appointments were brutal. Mike would sometimes take a day off to drive me to the city. At other times, friends or one of our visiting family members—most often my mother-in-law, Roberta, or my mother, who frequently visited from Florida—would make the trek with me. Following treatment I was often in too much pain to make it back home, so we would stay the night with Mike's parents.

I never explained to my family and friends that their sadness for what I was enduring triggered guilt in me and sent my emotions spiraling downward. It broke my heart to watch the reactions of those I loved. I vowed my independence and fought to find a way to manage this treatment alone.

When no one was available to drive me to appointments, I would try to make it on my own. At those times, I calculated that if I took a dose of pain medication just before leaving the house, sat on a generous amount of ice to reduce pain, and if traffic was light, I could make it halfway to the Bay Area before my symptoms overwhelmed me. Halfway there, I would pull off the freeway and into a parking lot. I would replace ice bags with extras I kept in my little cooler, lie down in the back of our SUV, and try to get control of my pain before going farther.

Heavy traffic spelled trouble. Several disastrous gridlock jams ended with me in the back of our SUV in a Home Depot parking lot writhing in pain, hysterical and overwhelmed. No matter what I tried, I could not do it alone. I would be reliant on my friends and family, and they would be subjected to my suffering.

⇥⇤

After six months it became evident that trigger point and physical therapy were no longer effective. Suspecting my pudendal nerve was the problem, Dr. West recommended a more aggressive approach involving a sequence of trigger point injections at the site of the pudendal nerve, three days a week for four weeks. This approach could possibly give me some relief for up to a few weeks if the nerve responded well. The pain from the injections was more brutal than anything I had previously experienced, and I thought about how desperate I had become to subject myself to a steady regime of torture.

Kian and I stayed at my in-laws' house during the four-week ordeal so I could have bed rest between injections. At the end of the first week of injections, I experienced some relief—my pain levels dropped by more than 30 percent. The torture rou-tine appeared to be making a positive difference. Along with the physical pain relief, I began to feel hopeful. *What if this treatment worked? What if I could sit for even a few minutes without pain?*

I fought an all-consuming daily battle with pain, treatment, and medical bills. The cost of my treatment was staggering. Dr. West was not contracted with my insurance company to pro-vide services; as a result, we were fully responsible for the cost of each visit. The bill for a single visit to Dr. West was more than eight hundred dollars, resulting in more than four thousand dollars a month in charges to my credit card. With our savings wiped out from previous surgeries and a mountain of medical bills facing us, my family members jumped in again and helped us pay for my visits with Dr. West.

Our financial struggles proved to be a training ground for me, because it was through them that I learned to navigate the health insurance business. After months of attempting to engage our insurance company in a discussion about our medical bills, I developed a system to escalate my case from the call screener to the supervisor level. The key to my approach was persistence.

I would call my insurance company, sometimes dozens of times a day, until my call landed with an agent who sounded fed up and ready to quit his or her job. With the agent's frustration and exasperation encouraged by my sympathetic ear, the care-fully scripted agent might then deviate from the strict protocol, which required that every request for reimbursement be denied.

Let's call one such agent Kirby. I took it as a gift from God when I got Kirby on the line after my eighth call of the day. I gave him my name, insurance number, and a call back number in case we got disconnected—I knew the drill.

"Okay, Mrs. Moody, how can I help?"

I launched into a litany of complaints. "Kirby, I see a specialist in San Francisco who is out of network. I am in agony 24/7 with a condition called pudendal nerve entrapment. I spend most of my day on the phone with this insurance company instead of resting. I have thousands of dollars of unpaid reimbursable medical claims—I have been submitting them for months—and according to the PPO plan we are entitled to a 50 percent reimbursement of the qualified expense.

"I log seven to eight calls per day to rectify this problem alone. So far, I have been promised by every agent that the reimbursements are submitted and being processed. In the meantime, I have received exactly diddly-squat."

The beeping tone of the recorded line droned every fifteen seconds.

"Wow. I'm so sorry you are suffering like this and there hasn't been any help for you. It's ridiculous that people as sick as you have to call this many times and still nothing gets done. Can you hang on a second? Let me scroll back to look at the notes in your file."

Kirby seemed not to care he was on a recorded line.

"Mrs. Moody?"

"Yes, I'm still here."

"I can't believe how many times you've called! The logs go back fourteen pages—with all the detailed notes of your requests for reimbursements. I even see the cross-references of the hard copies you mailed because you said the faxed copies were not getting processed."

"Yep. Welcome to my world, Kirby. Are you having fun yet?"

"I am not having fun. In fact, I can't stand the way this company does business, and I gave my notice. They treat us like crap. Obviously, you have been treated the same."

I was taken aback by his candid response, having grown accustomed to speaking to robotic insurance people.

"Uh . . . yeah, it has been less than pleasant dealing with this company," I said and smiled, wishing I could get a copy of the recording of our conversation.

"Mrs. Moody, as I read through the details in page after page of notes, there are bolded and capitalized directions here from all the different reps you've spoken to, but the claims adjustors are ignoring them. They're not scrolling back to read the complex history. I know a way to get them to look at the previous information so the claims will get processed."

"How's that?" I said with an audible exhale.

"I'm going to type 'hot sex' at the bottom of the page in large font. That will get their attention. They'll scroll through your record and eventually read the instructions."

"You're a genius, thanks."

"Pitiful what we have to resort to just to get you some help," he answered. "If you have other questions or concerns for the next two weeks, call me and I'll try to help you. I'm leaving after that."

He gave me the direct-dial number of his extension—a serious breach in insurance land.

Way to go, Kirby!

I spoke to Kirby only one other time, after which I was informed by the operator that I couldn't request to speak to a specific agent. Kirby left the agency, just as he said he would—but not before giving me the name and phone number of the head of the claims division. I thanked God for Kirby's compassion and prayed God would bless him wherever he landed. I loved this guy!

I received my first reimbursement payment from the insurance company two weeks later. What a weird world.

Thereafter, whenever new problems would arise concerning my claims, I would call Jerry, the division supervisor. Puzzled that I had his number, he soon grew weary of my many daily calls and personally authorized my claims to be processed correctly.

9

God Speaks

*Remember this. When people choose to withdraw far from a
fire, the fire continues to give warmth, but they grow cold.
When people choose to withdraw far from light, the light
continues to be bright in itself but they are in darkness.
This is also the case when people withdraw from God.*

—AUGUSTINE

As the months rolled on, our family and friends continued
to come from all over the country to help care for us—
babysitting Kian, yard work, meal prep, laundry, and countless
other things. They prayed for me, supported me, and made me
laugh, but the worry I saw in their eyes confirmed what I already
knew: I was not getting better.

One afternoon, when my dear friend Michelle was visiting from Los Angeles, she came out of the shower wrapped in
a towel to where I was splayed out on the couch feeling sorry

for myself. I could see she had been crying. I knew she had been steadily praying for me during her stay. She told me that while in the shower she had heard from God and had to deliver the message right away before she chickened out.

"I'm afraid when I say what I am supposed to say to you that we will no longer be friends."

Anger parked itself just below my hairline, and I could feel defensiveness rise up within me.

"You'd better go ahead and say it."

Michelle trembled as she spoke through her tears, "This pain is not your persecution, Jo, it is a gift from God."

"My gift?!" I raged. "What are you talking about?" Tears of fury flooded my eyes.

"I don't know how it is a gift, but I know it isn't God persecuting you."

I collapsed in a heap, sinking deeper into the couch, and sobbed even harder.

Michelle began to pray. As she prayed, I became aware of how much anger and resentment toward God I had kept bottled up inside. The truth she spoke blew off the cork that had held it back for so long. The more she prayed, the more I felt my spirit release the conviction I had held for so long that God was the cause of my torment and loss.

I prayed He would forgive me and bring about a complete change in my mind-set. I chose in that moment to believe pain could truly be a gift. Without supernatural intervention I never could have agreed with this new perspective. My weeping quieted as I felt myself humbled in prayer.

Because of Michelle's courage and faithfulness that day, I could give my struggle to God. Although things were far from rosy going forward, my viewpoint changed. I realized that I had fallen into the trap of comparing my life looking forward to the life I had known in the past, and I resolved to be present in the moment.

The cry of my prayer changed in that moment from one of self-focus: "God, help me. Please take away this pain. I'll do anything, just please take it away" to God-focus: "Lord, let my strength come from You only, not from myself. In Your place and in Your time, I know that You will heal me. Until that time, please make me what I should be within this trial, and help me to find joy in even the darkest of moments."

I could only attribute my resolve and accompanying sense of peace to the Holy Spirit.

I didn't know the upheaval I would face in the journey ahead and how many times I would be brought back to this moment when the Lord taught me to choose to give the struggle to Him. Such a simple concept, and yet profoundly difficult amid unrelenting pain.

Heidi and Rolland Baker express it well in core value number four of Iris Ministries:

> We understand the value of suffering in the Christian life. Learning to love requires willingness to suffer for the sake of righteousness. Discipline and testing make saints out of us and produce in us the holiness without which we would not see God's face and share in His glory. With Paul we rejoice in our weakness for when we are weak we are strong.[1]

≫≪

---

1. http://www.irisglobal.org/about/core-values.

By mid-2004, I had undergone nerve blocks, spinal injections, internal and external physical therapy, acupuncture, hormone treatments, medications of all types, biofeedback sessions, TENS Unit stimulation, nerve ablation, Prolotherapy, osteopathic manipulation, massage therapy, chiropractic care, and more. Nothing abated my pain.

As my pain levels increased, so did my need for higher levels of opiate medication. My medication management proved more than my primary care doctor was willing to handle, and a pain management clinic took over. Being treated like a drug addict because of the volume of the narcotic medications I needed left me feeling degraded and demoralized. *God, why should I be treated like a criminal when I need these drugs to survive? Please help me,* I prayed.

A few months later, I knew it was God's intervention when I became a patient of Dr. Greer's, an amazing Christian physician who not only wanted to manage my pain medications but had a deep desire to see me healed. He prayed with me at my appointments.

Thank you, God.

Dr. Greer put together a list of colleagues and respected department heads of leading hospitals and medical schools he believed would offer me the best chance of recovery.

"Joanne, if you are willing, I'd like you to see as many of these doctors as we can get approval for from your insurance company. You are too young to live like this, and with the high dosages of opiate medication in your system there is bound to be liver toxicity down the road. I want to make sure we've exhausted every avenue."

My stomach heaved.

"I truly appreciate what you are trying to do, Dr. Greer, but

I'm so tired of being mistreated and seeing medical professionals who don't have a clue about what's wrong with me."

My bottom lip was shaking, and tears stormed my eyes. Dr. Greer leaned forward and put his hand on my arm. I was shaking all over.

"Will you trust me? I will send you only to the physicians I know personally. I'll call each of them first and explain what you've been through."

His compassion and concern for me was evident, and as he spoke I could feel the peace of God descend on me.

True to his word, Dr. Greer gained insurance approval for me to be examined by the department heads of neurology, gynecology, urology, and orthopedics of the leading hospitals and medical schools in the Sacramento region. Some of these physicians were perplexed by my condition, while others had theories that involved more surgeries. In follow up to these appointments, I received reams of printed reports, medical opinions, and test results, but nothing else. None of them had ever seen a condition like mine.

In the ensuing months, I was haunted by flashbacks of all the years of treatment and pain, all the wasted money and time. Hopelessness settled on me like black fog. I took my eyes off Jesus again and let my mind wonder how much longer I could endure the unending torment.

Mike had just lost his job. Under the insurance coverage at the time, I couldn't qualify for other medical insurance, and we couldn't afford the COBRA payments to keep the insurance we had. One of my narcotic pain medications alone cost twelve hundred dollars per month. The rest of my medications would bring our monthly out-of-pocket cost to three thousand dollars. The figure became staggering as I added in our mortgage and living expenses.

※

Almost a year after Michelle and I had prayed, when I had given everything over to God, I was now out of options, money, patience, and coping skills. Mike stayed up through much of the night looking for jobs online. In the morning, he'd be bleary-eyed and agitated.

"Honey, I don't know how we're going to make it. I've got to find another job, but you can't be without insurance!"

I agreed with Mike, but a dump-truck load of guilt and frustration fell on me, preventing me from responding. I was not only culpable for our debt, I couldn't do anything to alleviate it. Kian, however, remained the light of our lives. At age five, he memorized full scenes from children's movies and would dress up in costumes and act out all the characters while Mike and I marveled at him. He was pure joy. His sweet nature and sense of humor were balm to my frayed life.

Yet, even though this child of ours gave me hope, thoughts of suicide returned like the unrelenting waves of a sea. Up to that point, they had come to me in fleeting moments when I could not find relief from pain for long periods of time. But now, unable to sleep most nights, I filled the bathtub with scalding water to distract myself. Lying submerged, my tears salted the bathwater as I tried to rein in my thoughts from the edge of the abyss.

If I took the whole bottle of sleeping pills, I might not ever wake up. That seemed like the only solution. Mike would move in with his parents, I reasoned, and they would help raise Kian. I contemplated how my side of the family would interact in Kian's life. I was so tired of hurting that I felt certain they would all figure it out somehow.

One day, with Kian in preschool and Mike at a meeting about a possible job, I went into my bedroom and began to pray. I had been contemplating suicide daily for several weeks and was desperate to hear something from God. That morning, after reviewing all the scenarios for how I could end my life, I had come up with a time frame and plan that involved sleeping pills plus some other medications.

When I tried to read my Bible and asked God to forgive what I was about to do, I was interrupted by an audible voice: "If you swallow all the pills in your possession, you will not die. Your pain in this moment seems unbearable to you, but if you abuse your gift of life, the outcome will be far worse for you. I am here always. You must not lean on your own understanding. Trust in Me and you will find true life."

The voice brought me to the floor. I was facedown on the carpet, paralyzed. As I shook with fear, I was engulfed in indescribable love. The powerful voice was filled with mercy, and I knew the Lord had spoken.

A picture flashed into my mind. I was lying in a hospital bed unconscious. Mike and members of our family were crying in the hospital corridor. I knew then that what I was seeing would be my reality if I chose to ignore His voice. I lay on the floor with my face pressed into the carpet.

I heard the voice again: "Fear nothing, for I am with you. You may continue to go to doctors for your comfort, but I will be the One to heal you. When you are healed, there will be no question in any person you encounter, that I AM the One who heals."

A profound awareness rose within me. This journey I was on was going to go according to God's will and perfect timing. I had to trust Him in everything, persevere through my pain and circumstances, and stop leaning on my own plan and understanding.

10

Mystery Solved

In modern medicine, we have a name for nearly
everything, but a cure for almost nothing.

—CHARLES F. GLASSMAN, AUTHOR OF *BRAIN DRAIN*

After many months of unemployment, Mike landed a great
job. We sold our house to help with my monthly medical
expenses and rented an apartment for a time. With Mike's new
job we eventually bought a house in a neighboring town. All of
this moving brought a brigade of family and friends to pack and
unpack us.

Kian rolled along through the chaos undaunted. He pretended the ottoman was a drum and kept time to the music as
my mom played the piano. He drew his grandparents, aunts,
and uncles into his games. All of us loved to hear him laugh.
Nevertheless, we were acutely aware of Kian's exposure to the

atmosphere of constant pain and fear. I prayed daily that he would have no lasting scars. When I watched his happy inter-actions with our families and friends, it gave me hope that he would grow up unaffected by my limitations.

In late-2004, I was sent to have a pudendal nerve latency test to measure the response of my pudendal nerve. With this test, my doctor could determine if there was a delay or deficiency in the nerve. Normal pudendal nerve terminal motor latency is 2.2–3.0 milliseconds or less. Measuring different points along the nerve would give a better picture of the damage and dysfunction of the nerve. The right and left nerve branches extend to the bladder, bowel, and sphincter muscles, all highly sensitive areas. Dr. West had avoided this excruciating test because my pain was already at intolerable levels. Since he had no other treatment options for me than to continue nerve blocks, Dr. West sent me for the testing to gain more information.

The test results were staggering. Against the normal motor latency response time of 2.2–3.0, my right side measured at 3.8. My left side score was 9.

"Mrs. Moody, you can see the left pudendal nerve is highly affected, but Dr. West will need to go over these results with you. He is the expert," the doctor said. I was still crying from the ordeal and could only nod. The nurse helped me off the table and into my clothes.

Heart racing and trembling, I held the walls of the corri-dor on my way out to keep from falling. I knew this confirmed pudendal nerve entrapment.

Mike drove me back to San Francisco to meet with Dr. West to review the test results. Although my doctor was always happy to see me, his eyes expressed concern at the latest findings.

"This is confirmation of PNE, but it is not what I had hoped for you," he said. "Surgery is the only thing left to give you some relief."

The word *some* screamed at me like a siren.

Dr. West continued. "Since American doctors are a good ten years behind the French in treating pudendal nerve entrapment, my recommendation is to have your surgery with the most experienced surgeon available—in France."

My ears rang, and Dr. West's voice sounded farther away. *I can't do more surgery. I can't. I could barely make it to the Bay Area; how would I travel to France?* We had no money for another surgery, and all the travel expenses would be unfathomable. My heart skipped a beat as it raced out of control.

I could barely whisper. "What kind of odds do I have for getting better?"

"There is a very good French physician, Dr. Bedeau. He is an ob-gyn and has specialized in pudendal nerve decompression surgery for more than ten years. The results he is publishing with his team look very promising."

"What does that mean for me?"

"Dr. Bedeau would have to tell you more about that, Joanne, but you need to know I wouldn't send you anywhere for surgery if I thought there was anything else that could help you."

All I could think about was the seven unnecessary surgeries and failed medical treatments I had already endured.

God, please. Don't let this work out if I am not supposed to have this surgery. I can't take any more.

I forced myself to swallow hard and reengage.

"Okay, I can't figure out how any of this can happen, but I would like to contact Dr. Bedeau so I can learn more."

"He speaks English, and I will arrange for you to e-mail him your questions, and then we'll set up a phone call when you're ready. The recent data he has recorded show that his patients diagnosed within a month to six months of the nerve becoming entrapped have been able to achieve 86 percent improvement."

"Eighty-six percent? Are those patients like me? Did they have all the surgeries and complications?"

"Your case is extensive, Joanne. I don't know what the percentage of improvement will be for you, but I know you deserve some quality of life, and I believe this is the best chance you have to at least reduce your pain levels," he said as the nurse readied the room for my nerve block.

Dr. West's stance had always been anti-surgery, and I trusted him completely. We had formed a unique friendship framed by satirical humor to offset the tension created by the treatment modalities he had inflicted and I had suffered through. There was nothing normal about any of it, but we tried our best. I knew he desperately wanted me to get better.

He had resorted to giving me nerve blocks inside my vaginal canal when the trigger point injections and physical therapy stopped working after month four. The nerve blocks had to be done without anesthesia and as close to the nerve canal as possible. I submitted to them because of the chance that one would hold for a few days, reducing my pain from a level ten to a seven. I was desperate for even a small break in the pain cycle that haunted me around the clock.

Although Dr. West had told me that the blocks were incredibly painful, nothing could have prepared me for the experience. I yelled and dissolved into hysterics with the first one. I could not breathe. Pain erupted in my pelvis like a firecracker exploding, and I nearly blacked out. Within a few minutes a flood of relief would come as the local anesthetic began to take effect.

No matter how many times I had the nerve blocks, I was

never prepared for the level of torment caused when the needle went in. In this barbaric procedure, pain determined the success of the block. I always told myself I wouldn't cry, but I always did. As I steeled myself for the needle, a thought flitted heavenward: *God, if I could have the surgery and it was successful, I wouldn't have to endure these any longer.*

When it was over, the nurse helped me dress and then went to get Mike from the waiting room. An invitation was never extended to Mike to come into the treatment room. Maybe the doctor knew better than to invite a spouse into such a difficult environment. I was glad for the unspoken rule. I don't think I could have endured Mike watching me in that level of pain.

I was shaking as I limped from the room with my ice bags inside my pants. Mike helped me down the hallway with tears in his eyes. "Oh Jo, I am so sorry. How can you keep suffering this way? There's got to be some help for us somewhere."

I couldn't respond as it took every ounce of resolve for me to keep moving forward to the elevator.

Thirty minutes from Sacramento, my pain subsided enough that I could tell Mike about my conversation with Dr. West.

"Dr. West confirmed pudendal nerve entrapment on the left side like we thought. He wants to send me to France for surgery because they are ten years ahead of American doctors, and I am scared to death." Mike looked at me in the rearview mirror.

"France? You can't even get to San Francisco, honey. How can you go to France?"

"I don't know, but all those papers you carried out with you have the information about pudendal nerve entrapment and the surgical approaches. We need to read everything we can about it."

Mike asked all the questions I was thinking about. "We've got to research this. Maybe you can speak with some patients who have already had surgery performed by this doctor and find out how they are doing. Do you know how much any of this costs? Does our medical insurance cover it? Jo, we'll find a way. If this is what you need to give you relief then this is what we'll do."

I wished I could sit up and reach over the seat to hug my husband. Instead I cried and nodded.

More important than gathering information about the procedure from Internet sources, I decided to take up the issue of surgery with God. Again and again I asked Him to close the door on this idea if I was not to pursue it. I knew I wouldn't be able to cope with another failed surgery. I was counting on Him.

⁂

Because pain remained such an issue for me at night, I often awoke long before dawn. In those early-morning hours, I discovered being on my knees was less difficult than lying flat. Day after day and year after year, I learned to seek God and hear Him more clearly. His comfort came as I drew near. When I entered His rest, I experienced gratitude and an ability to praise Him. The Spirit of God would overcome the torment of my flesh.

King David described seeking God early in the morning in Psalm 63. I learned the Hebrew word for *earnestly* as used in verse 1 literally means to seek the Lord early in the morning. David feasted on God and broke out in songs of praise and thanksgiving. He described thinking of God throughout the day and into the night as he lay on his bed to sleep.

Although I was not anywhere near the thankfulness and praise level of David, I did experience the Holy Spirit in those moments. Each encounter threw me a lifeline of hope. With every breakthrough I learned to know the Lord more in the midst of my pain.

Mike and I missed being part of a church, but how could we attend when I could sit or stand for only a few minutes at a time? What church would welcome me to lie down on the floor in the back?

We attempted to go a few times and found out the answer: *none*. In two churches, I was asked to find a seat, as they could not have me block the aisle or exit doors. There was no other place to lie down but aisles and exit doors. In another church, people around us glared at me for not standing during worship. So, we watched Charles Stanley on TV most Sunday mornings, but my own Bible reading and the communion with the Holy Spirit gave me the courage to face another day.

During the next few months, I researched websites and contacted several patients, both in the United States and in France, who had had the pudendal nerve decompression surgery. Only five surgeons in the world specialized in this type of surgery. All, except the surgeon who Dr. West recommended, used various surgical methods to access the pudendal nerve. Each technique cut through the sacrotuberous ligament. The patients I corresponded with who had this ligament cut now suffered from back pain. In addition, they received little relief from the original nerve pain. That was less-than-awesome news.

I corresponded with three women who had been in France for surgery three to five months earlier. Their news encouraged me. They gave me detailed descriptions of their surgeries, how they were healing, and the e-mail addresses for others who were six months ahead of them. I began to correspond with women who were up to ten months into the healing process. One patient claimed she was 95 percent better. She was out walking every day and had recently returned to work. Hope rose within me. Armed with information, I exchanged e-mails with the doctor in France.

Doctor Bedeau sent me information outlining the statistics and surgical approach of his team. I read and reread that the patients who had undergone release of the entrapped pudendal nerve were 86 percent better on average. Incredible news. I tried to moderate my feelings about the information. Part of me wanted to get up and dance—if that were possible—while another part of me refused to hope at all.

My internal dialogue exhausted me. *Could this finally be the answer? No, all the surgical interference and misdiagnoses does not make me a good candidate for the procedure. But what if God is opening this door to healing, and I can have relief from pain? I have to try. No, you can't make the journey to France, and, besides, where are you going to get the money?*

Round and round I went for days swinging between hope and despair—I finally forced the internal discussion to close and prayed. "Father, in the name of Jesus, if this is Your will for me, please work it out for me to go. I will know Your answer by Your peace and provision. Please help me to trust You no matter what Your answer."

My next trip to San Francisco included another lengthy discussion with Dr. West about the very real possibility of my having surgery in France.

"It's your best possible chance," he said. "I have seen Dr. Bedeau present his statistics at the pelvic pain symposiums, and I am sufficiently impressed with his results. I have sent several patients there, and although it is too soon to tell how much improvement they'll have, I am extremely optimistic they will be much better than they were before surgery. There are no other options available for you, Joanne. If you will consider surgery again, Dr. Bedeau would be the only one I would recommend to do it."

As I maneuvered the ice bags under me to a more comfortable position, I prayed. Once again I turned it over to God. I wasn't ready to do a somersault—not that I could actually do a somersault—over the idea of having yet another surgery. The thought of another failed, invasive, painful surgery terrified me. On the other hand, if there was anything medically out there that could help me, even a little bit, how could I not try?

Mike and I examined the statistics together and discussed the options before us.

"You know I support you. What do you want to do?" Mike said.

Tears welled in my eyes, and my voice broke. "I'm afraid to get my hopes up, and I'm frightened about another surgery. I am so sick of being the reason we are drowning in debt. Even if I wanted to go through this, I don't know how we'd pay for it."

Mike's shoulders slumped forward, and with a huge sigh he moved down to the floor where I was lying and folded his arms around me.

"I don't know what to do anymore. I wish I could just fix all of this and take away your pain. If you decide you want to try this, we'll figure something out about the money. I just want you to be well."

I responded with a flood of tears, tears of hope and tears of fear. *Okay, God, it's up to You.*

During the next week, I called each of my family members and told them what Dr. West had proposed. Although everyone was as guarded as Mike and I were, they agreed it was my best chance and my only chance.

≫✦

We spent months preparing a two-inch binder filled with evidence supporting the necessity of having the surgery done in a way as to preserve the sacrotuberous ligament. The basis of my argument was since the only doctor in America who performs the surgery routinely cuts through the ligament, I needed to go to France. The insurance company denied my request because the surgery was out of the country. My caseworker told me that while we had proved the need to keep the ligament intact, the insurance company maintained a strict policy against funding surgeries outside the United States.

With the insurance company's decision, I thought the door to France was closed. God had other plans, however. During the next few weeks I received calls and letters from family members and friends wanting to donate the money for my surgery and expenses. My sister Bev and her husband even held a fundraiser for me. I was overwhelmed by the outpouring of love and generosity.

God, You're here. You're in this. You're making a way. Thank You for answering my prayers.

The phone rang. Caller ID told me my sister Patty was on the line. Before I could say hello, Patty's excited voice reached my ears.

"Hey! You are not going to believe this, but my friend Sheila speaks fluent French and she wants to go with us and be our interpreter. She says we need an interpreter to get you the best care. Do you know she used to live in France and was a nanny for some people?"

Before I could respond, Patty continued, "She is taking

vacation time from her job to come with us and leaving her one-year-old at home with her husband ."

"I don't even know what to say. Wow. Yes. Thank you. I can't believe it."

"I have a great feeling about all of this, Joanne. This is going to be the thing that works. I'll organize it all with Bev."

Both my sisters and my brother, David, offered to go with me. The sisters, however, vetoed David's offer; his wife and young baby needed him at home. Bev and Patty, with college-age kids, decided they should be the ones to go. My mom and mother-in-law had been with me through all the other surgeries. My sisters and I agreed they shouldn't have to endure this surgery along with its strenuous journey. My two moms had withstood more than enough already.

The team of Bev, Patty, and Sheila offered me some relief from the anxiety I felt from being the cause of so much worry to my two moms. The whole thing came together so quickly, I believed it had to be divine intervention. My emotions sailed from doubt to excitement. My hope soared at the prospect of finally being free from pain. My fear of the surgery often over-whelmed me. But, as I told my mom, if the surgery helped even 20 percent, I would say it was worth it.

I emailed Dr. Bedeau about my decision, and he scheduled a time for us to talk.

※

The following week I was up at 4:00 a.m. to speak with him at the appropriate time in France.

"Yes, hello, Joanne Moody. Very good to meet you here." His

accent was strong and his English pretty solid, but his kindness painted the foreground of our conversation.

"Hi, Dr. Bedeau. Thank you for being willing to speak with me. I know Dr. West sent all my medical information to you, and I need to know what kind of chance I will have of a decrease in pain if I come to France and have the surgery with you. Your published statistics claim 86 percent improvement. That's amazing."

"Yes, this information has been true for us and our team for more than ten years. Here is a difference from America. French patients are diagnosed within six months of symptoms. American patients have many surgeries before arriving here for surgery. The 86 percent is for French patients."

"So 86 percent wouldn't apply to me then, I guess."

I felt fear creep up my neck.

"This is true, Joanne. Your case is difficult, but we believe much improvement for you. I don't have a percentage until my team can meet you and examine test results."

He gave me several dates to consider for the surgery. After I discussed the times available with Mike, my sisters, and Sheila, we set the date for April 2005.

Sheila handled all correspondence with Dr. Bedeau's secretary and smoothed all communication. Her involvement was key, and I thanked God for her even before we met face-to-face. Because so much can be lost in translation, I needed Sheila and her expertise every step of this journey. I didn't fathom just how pivotal her role was until much later.

It was settled. I was committed to another surgery. But now fear about what I might experience came over me in waves. During the day, I felt like I could control my thoughts, but the night was something altogether different. I had to deal with heart palpitations, cold sweats, and night terrors. I would often wake up with the feeling of being strangled or suffocated. When I could just think the name of Jesus, the terror would leave and the heaviness would lift off me.

I didn't want to worry Mike any more than I had to, so I didn't tell him about my battle with fear. I turned to Scripture for strength. I read *The Message* version of Psalm 62:11 and received comfort from David's understanding of God: "Strength comes straight from God."

11

The Journey to France

*Why do you go away? So that you can come back. So that
you can see the place you came from with new eyes and extra
colors. And the people there see you differently, too. Coming
back to where you started is not the same as never leaving.*

—TERRY PRATCHETT, FANTASY AUTHOR

Five days before I was slated to take off from Boston to France,
I was set to fly out early from Sacramento. With traffic we
hadn't bargained for, Mike and I were a little late in arriving at
the airport. I entered the terminal, pulling a suitcase with one
stuck wheel and carrying my infamous blue cushion: a square
pillow with the center cut out, designed for people with pudendal nerve entrapment.

I had discovered two years earlier that I could sit for three
to five minutes without a spike in pain if I used this hard-as-a-
rock cushion, off-loaded my weight onto my right buttock, and

perched on the very edge. I never went anywhere without it in the off chance I would have to sit for a minute or two. After five minutes, however, even my trusty blue cushion proved useless to combat the pain flare-ups.

My pulse rate spiked as if I had just sprinted to the top of the Empire State Building. I took a shaky breath, stepped between the stanchions, and moved onto the red carpet for the first-class line. I had used all the earned mileage points from our credit card purchases (most were charges for my treatments with Dr. West) for a first-class ticket, with hopes that the flight might be more bearable. Mentally, I tried to prepare myself for the challenge of sitting for six hours to get to Boston. Dread filled my empty stomach. I broke out in a cold sweat at the thought of enduring the long flight and checked my carry-on again for the vials of painkillers I brought with me.

First class had exactly three people in line. I glanced at the clock and realized I had forty-five minutes before my flight took off. I bit my lip and waited. I shifted my weight from one leg to the other to avoid the escalating pain. The couple in front of me were taking forever to book their travel arrangements to Beijing. They were traveling around the world and had a million questions for the agent. Tick tock, tick tock. Pain seared in my pelvis, so I squatted down and balanced myself by holding on to my suitcase. Thirty minutes until takeoff. Cold sweat was now running down onto the waistband of my pants. Ten more minutes crept by.

Finally, the agent called me forward. I limped up to the counter and laid my documents in front of her.

"Ms. Moody, you will not be allowed to board your flight. Check in is a minimum of forty-five minutes before your scheduled flight."

"I've been standing in this line for twenty-five minutes," I said. "I still have twenty minutes until the flight takes off. This is a tiny airport, and the gate is just at the top of the escalator. I can make it."

"No, that's not possible. You must check in for your flight at least one hour prior to departure. It is now less than twenty minutes before departure, and we cannot load your baggage," she retorted.

"Send my bag on the next flight then, and let me go, please," I pleaded.

"That's not possible, Ms. Moody. As of 9/11, FAA regulations state that no baggage may be loaded onto a flight without its owner checked in on that same flight."

"No need to wonder who is winning the war on terror," I whined. "Why can't you just rush this one bag up and let me go? Please, I am on my way to France to have surgery, and this is extremely painful for me."

"There would be no additional stress, Ms. Moody, if you had arrived here one hour prior to departure. I'm sorry that the other two flights to Boston today are sold out. You can return tomorrow morning for this same flight—we have two first-class seats left."

"I guess I have no other choice then, do I?" I received a negative shake of the head from Ms. Congeniality. "I suppose I better arrive two hours prior to departure tomorrow so this doesn't happen again."

"That's not necessary Ms. Moody, two hours prior only applies to international flights. Have a good day."

Already things were going wrong. Okay, this was a bad sign. I wheeled my bag out of the airport with my heart thumping in my chest and steam rising from my ears. Maybe I was making a terrible mistake in trying to go at all.

I called my sister Patty with a full ten minutes before the plane was set to take off.

"Hey, it's me," I burst into sobbing frustration and tried to repeat the details of why she would not be picking me up in Boston.

Patty responded with optimism. "Hey, no big deal! Just get on the plane tomorrow, and pretend today didn't happen. We have four days before the flight to France. It'll be fine. I'll pick you up tomorrow. Go home and lie down."

"Okay," I said, wiping snot on my sleeve.

After I called Mike on his cell, he found me squatting next to a concrete bench when he pulled up thirty minutes later.

"What a bunch of garbage this is," I said, as I crawled into the fully reclined passenger seat onto my stomach and stretched my legs behind me. "I'm sorry."

"No need to be sorry" he said. "We'll leave earlier tomorrow. I'm sorry this happened—9/11 made it such a pain for anyone to fly. I'll take you home to rest."

What rest? All I could think of was another twenty-four hours to lie around and worry about how I was going to get through the horrific ordeal in front of me. I tried to speak to God about my plight but couldn't concentrate.

The next day we arrived two hours early, and Mike hung out with me to make sure I made it onto the plane. This time things went without a hitch, mostly because no one in front of me was flying around the world with eighty-five bags to check. I made sure I had all my stuff with me, especially my other plane tickets, my driver's license, and the all-important passport. I patted my inside jacket pocket sixteen times in ten minutes just to make sure no one had pickpocketed me. I finally quit holding my breath. *I'm going.*

I turned to face Mike. "I guess this is it."

"It's all going to go fine. Kian and I are really going to miss you, and we'll be praying for you every day. Make sure you call me. And when you get out of surgery, make sure one of your sisters calls me with an update." He leaned in to kiss me.

"Yeah, okay. I'm really scared. I mean I know God has opened the door for this, but I'm so sick inside. I don't want to go through anymore stuff that doesn't work."

Mike folded me into his arms and hugged me. "Jo, we have to believe this will work. We have to trust that God lined all of this up so you can have relief. You can't go on like you are. Your sisters and Sheila are going to take great care of you. I'm counting on it."

I nodded through tears, kissed Mike once more, and started toward the boarding area.

∗≪

I settled into my first-class seat with my blue cushion. After takeoff I planned to recline my chair back as far as it would go and then, kneeling on the floor, lean across the front of my seat on my stomach, provided I didn't have anyone sitting next to me.

Wow. This might work out after all. Thank you, God.

I whipped out my cell phone to call my sister. "I'm actually on the plane."

"Congrats. Did you get set up in first class?" Patty asked.

"Yep."

"Any odd people sitting next to you?"

How well she knew my crazy tales of flying in the past. "Nope."

"You're kidding. Fabulous. I'll be there to pick you up. We're having a heat wave, so I'll be the one without clothes on at the baggage claim," Patty said. "Between the heat and these hot flashes, I'm the one who needs ice packs in my pants. Do you have extra?"

Patty was so wonderful and could always make me laugh—a bright spot in this dreary scenario. I snorted at her question before I hung up.

The nonstop flight was long, but no one seemed to mind my reclined chair, or my need to often flip my body and walk, kneel, and squat continually during the flight. When the flight attendant asked if I was all right, I quickly told her it was my back. She nodded sympathetically. I preferred to say it was my back rather than publicizing that my pain centralized in my pelvic floor, vagina, and anal cavity. Nothing shocked people more than when I told them I had fiery pain in my vagina and rear end. Commenting on my back rather than my pelvis ended the curious questions about my strange movements.

Once my flight landed, I limped around looking for my naked sister at baggage claim. She was right there fully clothed, and without a hint of sweat on her upper lip.

"Hey! You made it!" She greeted me with a hug.

"I'm so glad to see you! How hot is it out there?"

"It's brutal, but I've slathered myself with progesterone and wild yam cream over every inch of my body, so I don't think I'll get dehydrated for a few hours." She lifted her arm to me. "Feel my skin! Nobody told me that you turn into a total prune going through this menopause stuff. I'm like a lizard. I'd heard all about the vaginal dryness, but who cares about that? What about my face? Now I know my eyes are too big for my eyelids. They're drying up."

"Not to worry," I said. "I heard it's a gradual thing that lasts only ten years or so."

"Ten years? What? By next week you'll be able to pick up my ashes off the floor and blow me into the wind. I've already used three jars of that yam cream just this week."

We fell over laughing.

The next day I was elated to finally meet Patty's friend and our French interpreter, Sheila. Before I could say anything, I was wrapped in her warm embrace.

"Jo, I have heard so much about you from Patty that I feel like I already know you. You've been through hell, and I am so excited to be able to help in any way I can."

I stepped back to look into her eyes. "I don't even know how to thank you. Having you with us and knowing you can speak the language is the key factor for me deciding to go forward."

"I've been in touch with Dr. Bedeau, and he has my cell number, so we're all set. I love France. Since I lived there and worked as a nanny, I not only know the language but the culture too. That's really important."

"I know. We're all grateful since the only French we know is *croissant*, and we will likely offend everyone with our lack of etiquette," I said.

Patty snickered. I could see immediately why my sister and she were such good friends.

We chatted about our plans to get together early the following evening so that I could meet Sheila's husband. I told Patty we should take two cars because I'd never make it past seven because of my pain.

"It's like Mount Vesuvius down there when my meds start to wear off. Then if I take more meds, I need twice the sleep meds to help me sleep."

I hated this cycle of trying to navigate my life because of pain levels and medication.

"No worries," Patty said. "I can always tell when you're not doing well—your eyes glaze over and you get a weird expression on your face. We won't even need a signal for me to get you out of there. I'll just look at you and know."

"That's the power of sisterhood," I said and choked back a sob.

"Nope," she said, "nothing like that. It's the power of the circles under your eyes getting darker and darker when your pain is increasing."

Lovely. Maybe I need some yam cream under my eyes.

Friday morning, April 15, 2005, came. I both loathed and loved its arrival. Despite my wavering emotional state, we headed to the airport.

"We're going early because I'm paranoid about a repeat of my Sacramento airport experience," I announced. We rolled our bags up to the ticket counter.

"You've got your passports, right, you guys?" Patty asked.

"Right here!" Sheila and I said in unison.

Patty and Sheila checked in first, and I was next. I handed the agent my passport and my ticket. She immediately stopped short and stared at me. My stomach folded in half.

"Your passport name doesn't match your ticketed name. I can't let you on this flight," she said.

"*What?*" Patty and I said at the same time.

"Your passport says Joanne Miles and your ticket is printed Joanne Miles Moody."

I had looked at my passport before leaving home to make sure it hadn't expired. I had been so busy fighting the insurance company and the medical bills the weeks before my trip that I had overlooked the simple name change requirement on my passport. Since I had married Mike, legally Miles was now my middle name.

"But, my name is Joanne Miles," I said. "Can't you just drop the Moody from my ticket?"

"We cannot change the names on tickets once they've been purchased," said the agent.

My stomach did a somersault, and I started to cry. Patty and Sheila jumped into action.

"Where is your supervisor?" asked Patty.

"This is ridiculous. This woman is going to France for necessary surgery," Sheila said.

"Even if I get my supervisor, there is nothing to be done," said the agent.

"Well, we'll just see about that," Patty said.

"Call your supervisor immediately, please, so we don't miss our flight." Sheila's voice escalated in volume.

A portly middle-aged man entered the scene. Obviously prepared for battle, he swaggered over to us while trying to pull his pants up over his own excess baggage. My rising pain levels required that I squat, back braced against the ticket counter, while Patty and Sheila opened negotiations.

"Thanks for coming to speak with us," said Patty. "I'm Patricia Deyermond. My sister and our interpreter, Sheila Wiszt, are on our way to France where my sister will have critical surgery. This trip has been planned for a long time, and we have to get her there on this flight."

Bill sniffed and looked us over.

"Ms. Lang, let me see the passenger's passport and tickets please."

I noticed both Sheila and Patty crossing their arms.

"Well, it appears that your sister forgot to change her passport to include her married name. Now she has two different last names, and that's not okay with the TSA."

I attempted to stand up again. "I legally have two last names, sir. If you will just drop the Moody from my ticket, everything will match."

"We can't do that," he said, as the other agent smiled a little.

"Who is the person we need to talk to get the ticket name changed?" Patty asked.

Bill drew breath noisily through his nostrils again and smiled at Patty and Sheila. "That would be me."

"You make all these decisions for this airline?" Sheila asked.

"I am the manager of customer service, and, therefore, I am the one responsible for making these decisions, yes." He thrust his shoulders back and sniffed hard.

"Well, what kind of customer service are you providing here?" Patty's voice rose. "We have to get her to France—*today*. She has to have surgery. Look at her driver's license. It says Miles Moody. Look at these three credit cards! Each of them says Miles Moody. She has a wallet full of proof she is who she says she is— and you won't let her on the plane?"

As if he weren't there, Sheila said, "I don't think he actually has the authority. I think this is over his head, and he doesn't want to call another supervisor."

Bill's face turned bright red, and spittle formed at the corners of his mouth. The bottom button on his starched white shirt threatened to give way.

"All right, ladies, I will change her ticket name, but you will be in trouble when you are out of the country because her name will not change on all the legs of your flight. It's out of my hands outside this country."

"Whoa, wait a minute." Patty's loud voice meant business. "We are flying your airline the entire trip, and you can't make a name change in the computer?"

His mouth turned up ever so slightly in the corners. "Our European flights are contracted with Air France, and we can't change things in their system."

"Why can't you make a phone call then?" asked Sheila.

"Look, this is all I'm going to do for you, and I shouldn't even be doing this. You can take up your problem at customs when you arrive." He signed some piece of paper, handed it to the agent, and walked away.

"I wrote down his name and employee number," said Sheila. "I'm writing to the president of the airline. This is insane."

I was shaking when the agent handed me my reissued "Joanne Miles" ticket.

"Why does this nonsense keep happening to you?" Patty asked me as we headed toward our gate.

I was too nauseated to respond, and a wave of pain washed over me. Sheila handed me a tissue for my mascara, which had liquefied under my eyes.

Patty patted my back. "He was an idiot. We're not going to have any trouble in France or in customs. Sheila can talk to them."

12

Air to Ground

My fear of flying starts as soon as I buckle myself in and then the guy up front mumbles a few unintelligible words, then before I know it I'm thrust into the back of my seat by acceleration that seems way too fast and the rest of the trip is an endless nightmare of turbulence, of near misses. And then the cabbie drops me off at the airport.

—DENNIS MILLER, WRITER

I didn't believe for a second there was smooth sailing ahead. I tried to will myself into a state of joy but was at a loss for where to start. Patty looked at me, and I could see she didn't believe it was all going to be trouble-free from here on either, given my history of difficulty these past years.

The flight to France was long and arduous, especially since we were in the steerage portion of the aircraft. I walked up and down the aisles until I annoyed those around me. I had purchased two seats so that I could lie curled up on my side with my feet in Patty's lap.

Patty and Sheila slept a little while, I slept none and prayed a lot.

I wondered if the small fiasco at the airport indicated that perhaps I shouldn't go through with this surgery. *No*, I thought. *If I don't do it, I'll always wonder if this was the answer.* Back and forth my thoughts flew until we landed in Paris.

I took a handful of narcotics to get through the huge Charles de Gaulle Airport. We walked for what must have been a mile to get to our connection to Marseilles.

"No wonder the French are all so thin," I muttered, pressing on through the crowds.

We arrived at the small ticket counter to check in only to find my ticket invalid. The agent told Sheila that she and Patty were in the computer, but I was not. We learned that the name change in Boston had canceled my name from the log for my next flight.

"Here we go again," I said.

Sheila rattled off a slew of impressive French, and the agent said "oui" several times. I handed over my passport and driver's license. Sheila turned to face Patty and me.

"Our plane is close to boarding now, and since it is only half full the agent was able to get you a seat, Jo."

Patty sighed, grabbed the carry-on bag out of my hand and started walking. I was drained. *God, why is all of this happening? Maybe I missed You and this isn't Your plan for me at all.*

My pain levels soared to new heights, and I could feel my heart primed for explosion. All I wanted to do was close my eyes and disappear. I was so overcome with pain and emotion that I couldn't even pray.

"Let's get on this plane before anything else happens," Patty said, hustling us on board. "I think it would be good for all of us to take a break from the stress and sit apart."

Neither Sheila nor I had any objection. I spread out in an empty row and lay down, barely breathing.

God, are You there? Did I make a mistake? I prayed silently. I heard no reply as my tears slid down the green leather seat.

Once in Marseilles, we headed for the airport ATM. Sheila and Patty put their credit cards in and withdrew their money without a hitch. I inserted my card three separate times and received nothing except an error message. Patty inserted my card and then Sheila tried, but we all got the same error message. Exasperated by my pain and lack of sleep, I yanked another card out of my wallet. Again, nothing.

"Oh, my gosh! Can you believe this? Now I can't even get any money!"

Patty interrupted my rant. "You don't need any money. I'll take care of everything. Let's get to the rental car place."

"I appreciate that you want to take care of the money, Patty. I just need to be able to get money. It's the principle. Why aren't my cards working when yours are?"

"I don't know why—oh, yes, I do!—Because you're you, that's why!" she said.

And I knew she was right.

As we headed toward the terminal exit she rolled her eyes and said to Sheila, "Now isn't Joanne the most blessed person you've ever met?"

Sheila tried to smile at me reassuringly, but her eyes looked worried.

I sweated my way through customs while praying like mad there wouldn't be a problem with the name discrepancy on my

Air France stub. Despite my anxiety, the customs part went smoothly and I exhaled. *Maybe this will be a trend,* I told myself. The positive thought faded, when a mere ten minutes later my credit card mishaps continued at the rental car counter.

I told Patty I would rent the car using my credit card. Patty agreed that was a good idea to make sure my card was okay after the disaster at the airport ATM. Sheila spoke to the car rental agent in French. The agent seemed kind and exchanged smiles with each of us.

"Your French is very good, but I also speak English," she said.

I leaned over the counter and handed her my credit card. "Fantastic. I'd like to pay for the car rental," I said as the agent swiped my card.

"I'm sorry, Mademoiselle, this card is not acceptable." The corner of her mouth twitched.

Sheila raised her eyebrows while Patty didn't look surprised. Patty promptly handed over her perfectly acceptable card.

"May I use your phone to call the credit card company?" I asked.

"Oui," said the agent.

The call solved the mystery. My credit card company was concerned over my sudden overseas charges and, therefore, had frozen my account until I contacted them. To ensure my card was not stolen, I answered twenty questions to verify my identity and then received an apology from the company representative for the inconvenience.

"You have no idea," I said. "It just would have been nice if you had told me ahead of time this was a policy of yours. I've been a customer of yours for seventeen years."

"We don't tell our customers because that would give thieves more information to work with," said the agent.

"I don't think the good guys are winning," I told him and hung up.

Patty and Sheila rolled their eyes and then rolled our luggage out to our newly rented French automobile. Patty made a bed for me in the back seat in one of the largest cars the rental agency offered. It was slightly bigger than a two-seat Fiat with a small back seat. I lay on my side with my knees curled up and my face buried in a pillow. Patty drove and Sheila navigated. Meanwhile, I enjoyed the description of the lovely French countryside from their commentary. My heart ached to see some of it before we left France.

I sighed and tried to combat my self-pity with humor. "Maybe I can use my credit card and get a book with photos of the French countryside," I said.

"We'll buy you one," they said together. I let out another big sigh and swallowed yet another dose of painkillers.

When the meds kicked in, I figured out a way to balance with my hip on the pillow to catch a glimpse of the scenery while looking out the bottom edge of the window. I was overwhelmed by the beauty of the city of Aix-en-Provence, with its center plaza and ancient buildings. The town square was postcard perfect with a lovely fountain and street vendors selling French linens. For a few fleeting moments, I forgot why we were there and enjoyed the novelty of being a tourist in a stunning new land.

We followed the directions to the hotel and circled the block no less than ten times. Signs for the hotel were visible, but the entrance wasn't. Finally, Sheila phoned the front desk and was told how to enter. Patty maneuvered the small car into the hotel by making an almost complete U-turn, clearing a long iron railing running the length of a storefront, squeezing between large delivery trucks, driving down a one-way alley the wrong way, and—wow! We made it!

"I need Valium if I'm going to have to do this every time we go anywhere," Patty said, taking the luggage out of the car.

Patty was relieved to be out from behind the wheel. Sheila was elated to be speaking French. I was just happy to have made it at last.

Our room with three beds opened up to a view of the quaint buildings surrounding the hotel. Shutters in every color framed the windows of the mustard-colored building facing us. So French and lovely, the sensual experience included bakery smells wafting up from the street through opened windows. We told Sheila to call and order room service just so we could hear her speak more French. We marveled at how beautifully she spoke the language. She confided that locals thought she was a native, but her clunky American running shoes gave her away.

"I know they're all staring at me," she said.

"What's wrong with your shoes?" we asked in unison while venturing downstairs to the lobby to grab a map of the city.

"You'll see," Sheila said as she glanced around at every pair of feet in the lobby.

Patty and I noticed everyone wore very elegant shoes—leather, narrow, and low to the ground. Sheila was right. We could tell who was French by looking at their pumps, loafers, and boots. Comparing the elegance of French shoes to American running shoes was like comparing the supple movement of a leopard to a springy kangaroo.

Patty and I had on leather slides, and they were barely passing. We couldn't even say *bonjour* correctly, so our shoes were our only chance of not advertising our American identity. Sheila moved confidently in her white Nikes with the blue swoosh on the side. Her French could overcome any footwear.

I noticed I was wearing my pink scarf all wrong as I compared my clumsy attempts at fashion to the French women I saw in the lobby. I nearly choked myself trying to figure out how they made their scarves look so elegant. Oh, the unfashionable Americans, with the clunky shoes and improperly knotted scarf.

"This is too cool," Patty said, taking in our surroundings.

"Yeah, if we could just forget the part about why we came here, it'd be way cool," I said, trying to sound positive.

"Well, girls, if you're up for it, let's walk around the town a bit and get our bearings," Sheila said as she cinched her all-season jacket around her waist.

I decided to get more of my bearings in a prone position, so I didn't accompany the two scouts. I headed back to the room and tried to read for a while. It didn't settle me. I tried to pray, but my mind reeled from one fear to the next. Finally, I submitted to picking my fingernails and resigned myself to one undeniable fact: I was scared to death. I was thankful for the prescription sleeping pills I had refilled before the trip and looked forward to being put out of my misery after the sun went down.

A few hours later my two roommates returned.

"Oh, my gosh, Jo, you are not going to believe how beautiful it is! We ate paninis at this little café, and everyone is so French!" Patty's eyes sparkled.

Sheila jumped in. "We walked through these narrow alleys to get to the center square of the city. You know, that fountain we passed ten times when we were trying to find the hotel entrance? That's the center; it's gorgeous, and all around it are linen and perfume shops. I can't wait to go shopping!"

Listening, I was hoping to look around after dosing on the maximum number of painkillers the next day. I had two days before my hospital check in, but I had to meet with the surgeon, Dr. Bedeau, tomorrow evening and the day after with Dr. Vissar, who would do the preliminary nerve conductivity test.

Before turning off the lights, Patty and Sheila spread out maps and brochures they had collected on their walk around town. They decided tomorrow we'd go to a magnificent fifth-century village. Patty read me the description from the brochure closest to her.

"Moustier Saint Marie sits below a tapered notch at the base of rocky cliffs. It is a lovely village in a gorgeous setting. Moustier Ste. Marie sits astride a rushing mountain stream that divides the two halves with a narrow rocky canyon. The centerpiece of the village is a twelfth-century Notre Dame church topped by a four-tiered bell tower. The chapel is built on the site of an even older church dating back to the fifth century—"

"Wow. It sounds amazing but steep. I wonder if I can even walk around there." Just thinking about an increase of pain made me flinch.

"We've gotta do this, Jo. Even though it's a bit of a car ride, we'll set you up with your cushion and a pillow in the back seat. You can't come all this way and not see something besides the inside of the hospital," Patty said.

I knew I needed to escape from my strangulating thoughts and keep my mind focused on something else. I responded to Patty with a nod.

The next morning we set off for a magnificent day of sight-seeing. I lay in my makeshift backseat bed and was blown away by the beauty of the French countryside. Even from my vantage point at the base of the window, landscapes I had seen only in pictures and movies now paraded by me outside the car window. The village was breathtaking, and I felt much better after yet another round of narcotics and a brief walk around the town where the ground was occasionally level.

After lunch we headed back down the road the way we came. Sheila began reading about a little town called St. Remy, not far off our route, which she insisted we see on the way back to the hotel.

"I saw it in the brochures last night, and they say it's one we shouldn't miss! It's the quintessential French experience! Van Gogh painted *Starry Nights* there, and Nostradamus was born there. Better yet, they have perfume, linens, and French pottery." said Sheila. "How are you holding up back there, Jo?"

"Ready for the French experience," I joked. "Do you guys have a gurney in the trunk? I believe I bought the luxury package from Flat on Your Back Tours."

Sheila and Patty laughed.

"We could do that you know," Sheila said as her eyes lit up at the possibilities. "We could accompany other patients here from the States and make sure they enjoy some sightseeing as well as provide interpretation for their surgeries."

"You could do that, Sheila, but I'm going to finish my teaching degree, and Jo is going to be couch surfing for a good long while. But, it's a great idea. You should talk to Dr. Bedeau about it."

The quick stop in St. Remy worked wonders for my anxiety. The tangle of streets led us to a charming group of historic store-fronts with delightful shopkeepers inside. The smells of French room sprays and perfume was like a panoramic view for my nose—ocean breezes, a valley of wildflowers, rose petals crushed between finger tips. Every spray was unique. I wanted to stay there. Instead, I purchased a few gifts and headed to the car to lie down.

As I walked, the lush garden landscape revived hope in my

heart that this surgery would finally relieve me from my burden of pain. Maybe one day I will travel and see France without a gurney tour. My adrenaline shot up at the thought—or maybe it was just the caffe latte served in a cup the size of a soup bowl that I had just downed.

We were finally able to enter our hotel on the first try by late afternoon. This time Patty had to dodge only one large truck at the narrow entrance. No Valium needed.

I collapsed into bed while Patty and Sheila embarked on another journey by foot in search of dinner. They brought back what would become my staple: a delicious French panini. How could a sandwich with simply tomatoes, cheese, and bread taste this good?

I hoped the sandwich I ate would prevent my stomach from souring as the time neared for my appointment with Dr. Bedeau, but I was wrong. Weird as it was to us, at seven that evening, we walked past the Centre Hospitalier Avec Vue, which, according to Sheila, meant "hospital with a view," and around the corner to the doctor's office. I would be admitted to the hospital in two days, so we were glad to know it was so close.

We entered Dr. Bedeau's office, and Sheila immediately struck up a conversation with his nurse, Brigitte. They had been corresponding via e-mail for many weeks so both were happy to finally meet face-to-face. Patty and I just nodded and smiled, trying to hide our embarrassment at not being able to decipher one word of their conversation.

"At least our shoes look good," Patty whispered. I snorted with laughter.

We eventually headed to the magazine table where we pretended to understand what we were reading. A woman in her thirties and dressed in a tailored skirt and blouse peered at us over her magazine. When I looked at her, she looked away. An older woman sitting a few rows from us knitted while she waited. She seemed too intent on her needles to pay attention to us. It was nearing eight.

"Odd hours they keep, huh?" Patty said to me.

"Maybe the insurance companies are worse than in America and make them work crazy hours," I responded.

"The healthcare is free here," she whispered. "But, the fact is, we need to remember to bring towels and soap from the hotel to the hospital. Because of socialized medicine they don't provide that stuff."

With the stress of the trip I had completely forgotten France had socialized medical care.

"Well, at least we won't get charged seventeen bucks for a tongue depressor like in American hospitals," I muttered. "I hope they have the toasty blankets before and after surgery, though. That's the only good thing about surgery."

"We can whip some off the hotel beds and find a microwave," Patty teased.

A tall, blue-eyed, graying at the temples, fiftyish man in a white coat approached us with a beaming smile and extended hand.

"Bonjour! Bonjour, Madam Moody. It is so nice to finally meet you." Dr. Bedeau extended his hand to me and then turned to Patty. "This is your sister, yes?"

"Yes, this is Patty," I confirmed, feeling comforted by his demeanor. Sheila joined our little circle and exchanged French with Dr. Bedeau.

"He speaks English really well," I whispered to Patty.

He turned back to us. "Where is your other sister? She is coming as well?"

I nodded. "She's coming in a few days."

"A very good family and friends." Dr. Bedeau beamed. "This is so very good for the patient to become better."

"I'm grateful to have so much support. I couldn't have made this trip without all of them." My mind flashed back to the passport nightmare.

"It is a long journey, yes," he said.

"Please, will you come with me, Madam Moody? Madam Sheila and Madam Patty will stay."

I followed him into a small alcove just off the waiting room. Dr. Bedeau sat at a large desk with two chairs facing him. I knelt on the floor with my blue cushion under me while he asked many questions.

Finally, he lay down his pen and said, "I will do an examination before you see Dr. Vissar tomorrow morning."

"Okay, that's fine."

I glanced around for a door to an examining room but didn't see one. I saw only a short hybrid-type table in the alcove that somewhat resembled an examining table but at a forty-five-degree angle. *Is this the examining area? Where is the privacy?*

He stood up and gestured for me to follow him over to the table. My face contorted into one giant pinch, and my eyes searched his to try and pull meaning from his gestures.

"Please to get ready for my examination here."

His English was good, but I thought perhaps I misunderstood something. A few seconds passed as slowly as dripping molasses, until I got the gist of his brief instructions and hand signals pointing to the small table. *I have to take off my jeans and underwear right here in front of him and climb on to that table. Wow. Okay, that's new.*

After I shed my clothes and took a deep breath, I lay on the tricky table spread-eagle, minus a sheet, in front of the doctor scribbling on a notepad. I took mental notes. *It's obvious the French are very comfortable with their bodies. While here I'll have to abandon my prudish, American ways of covering my privates. Who knows? Perhaps after this surgery I'll be free enough to revive streaking at football games back home.* Thankfully, the painful exam didn't last long. Dr. Bedeau announced that he concurred with Dr. West's diagnosis of pudendal nerve entrapment.

"You will have a latency test done by Dr. Vissar tomorrow, so that we will know how much damage the nerve has at this time. The same test will be done again during and after the surgery, before you wake up, to be sure we have freed it all the way," he explained. "When the nerve impulse is in the normal range, then we are certain there is no more entrapment."

"I know you can't really answer this, but I have to ask it anyway," I said. "Will I be 80 percent better?"

"Of course, that is our hope," he said. "Our studies indicate a large number of our patients are 80 percent better within one year after surgery. But we do not have the misdiagnosis here in France for this condition as you do in America. Our patients here know almost right away when the symptoms start. They come here, have the surgery, and go home. They go back to their lives, and we don't see them again. We have been doing this surgery for ten years with very promising results.

"Since I have been doing the surgery on American patients for these two years, it is difficult to say the percentage of improvement. Most American patients have had the condition for many, many years. Almost all that I have seen have had multiple surgeries that make this condition more difficult. Your case is difficult. You have had many surgeries and many years with pain. We believe you will be better than now, but we cannot predict the percentage. Okay? We are hopeful!"

I nodded. I knew if I opened my mouth to speak, my eyes would flood. A shred of hope. That's all I had to hang on to.

"I will see you at the hospital the day after tomorrow for your surgery, but you will check into the hospital tomorrow afternoon, after you have visited with the anesthesiologist."

"Thanks, Dr. Bedeau. Thank you for pursuing this work and helping us," I said.

"I am happy to have such a great team of people to work with me here," he said.

What a humble man, I thought as I shakily moved off the table, slipped on my pants, and zipped up. I walked out of the alcove to meet Patty and Sheila.

"How'd it go over there?" Patty asked.

"He seems like such a nice man," added Sheila.

"I'm guessing you guys missed my 'show' back there on the table? Didn't you see me splayed out like today's catch at Pike Place Fish Market? I was raising my eyebrows to get your attention."

"Well, we did see some of you, but you were partially blocked by Dr. Bedeau."

"What a relief. I still have a shred of modesty left."

That was not to be the case in another twenty-four hours.

"Talk about embarrassing," Sheila said. "Remember, I told you guys I was a nanny for a while for this French family?"

We nodded.

"Well, I had been with them for about two weeks and was still not in tune with French etiquette. As far as medicine goes, the French administer most over-the-counter meds in suppository form. I know that now, but at nineteen, I had no idea. A few hours after dinner one night I was really nauseous. I asked the mother if they had something like Pepto-Bismol. She went to the bathroom and came back with something shaped like a Brazil nut but twice as long. I immediately bit it in half and began chewing like mad. My employer's eyes got as wide as saucers as she explained to me that it was a suppository! I was mortified!"

Patty and I doubled over laughing.

"So, Sheila, you better ask the anesthesiologist which end I'm supposed to use for my meds, so I don't repeat your performance."

Her laughter matched mine. "You can count on me."

13

Coffee to Go

In our rushing, bulls in china shops, we break our own lives.
—ANN VOSKAMP, AUTHOR OF *ONE THOUSAND GIFTS*

Early the next morning we tried to figure out how to get coffee to go. We could get coffee via room service and pay twenty-seven dollars for a carafe, but we were looking for a cheaper version of our morning java. Even Sheila found it difficult to convey our need to the hotel staff. They had never heard of someone wanting coffee to go, and we found out quickly the French do not have anything to go. Theirs is a life built on relationships, and those relationships are built around food, and food is not to be rushed.

We learned the French spend time with friends and family over a cup of coffee or two at a local café. They don't order a triple, double-whip mocha latte at the neighborhood Starbucks drive-through window on their way to work. They typically don't even drive to work, preferring to walk everywhere. We were the odd Americans in search of a good cardboard cup of coffee for our walk to my morning appointment with Dr. Vissar.

I swallowed more pain meds as we set out to walk the short distance to the doctor's office, hoping to find java somewhere en route. Bowels and pain pills make a nasty combo, proving coffee a necessary staple in my daily diet.

We wandered into town and passed a place with many patrons. As most of them were smoking, I didn't want to go in. Cigarette smoke made me gag, and I needed all the breath I could muster that morning. A short way down the street, we approached another place that looked like a nightclub, but, nevertheless, was open for business at 9:00 a.m.

We went in to see people drinking coffee and smoking all around us. The place had velvet settees with a silver stage curtain. I expected *La Cage aux Folles* to start at any moment. Some of the patrons looked as if they had rolled right from their martini-laden evening into the java-soaked morning in the same seat. Waiters in black pants, white shirts, and bow ties served us coffee in soup bowls without handles, flanked by slabs of French bread. I found out, unlike in America, liquor is served any time of day in France. This glittery palace doubled as a nightclub and coffeehouse. This would be big in America.

I stood and shifted my weight from leg to leg, then squatted and tried to perch myself on the edge of the chair. All the while I observed those around us, amazed by their carefree demeanor. I, on the other hand, was the antithesis of relaxed. No position came easily or without pain. To top it off, I burned the roof of my mouth trying to down the coffee as I looked out onto the street. Even there everyone appeared happy and stress free. "I bet the road rage here is minimal."

"Probably the only ones with road rage are the Americans looking for coffee to go," Patty said.

As we drained our bowls of coffee, our bill was presented in a nice leather case. Patty picked it up first. "Wow! Twenty-eight bucks for coffee and bread. That might be all the inspiration we need to kick the caffeine habit while we're here."

"Yea, I guess I can buy a giant bag of prunes instead," I said.

We found Dr. Vissar's office on the floor below Dr. Bedeau's, around the corner from the coffee nightclub. Once inside the waiting area I grew quiet. I knew what lay ahead, and the dread silenced me. Although a latency test is nothing like surgery, it's no picnic either.

Dr. Vissar came out and tried to pronounce my name in English. Sheila hopped out of her chair and began speaking to him in French. Sheila was proving to be invaluable, and I couldn't imagine the stress we would be operating under if she had not been there to translate for us.

The doctor invited me into the exam room. Although this one had a door that closed to the waiting area, I repeated the same routine as in Dr. Bedeau's office the night before. No privacy, no sheet, just spread-eagle on the table. Would I ever get used to this? I tried to detach myself from the scene while Dr. Vissar apologized for his lack of command of the English language.

"I think you speak quite well," I said.

"No, no, no, my English is no good," he said, holding up a hand.

"This will not have much pain," he said.

"That's very good English!" I told him. *Maybe he knows a different way of doing the test with no pain.* My hope increased.

"Why are you clipping that there?" I asked as he attached a

metal electrode device to my clitoris! "Are you kidding? This is not what we do in America!"

"We must use this spot due to nerve is most . . . how do you say . . . feeling? Here, this will not be painful," he said.

I suddenly felt cold and clammy. *How could he say this would not be painful?*

"We will start now, yes?" said the doctor.

I wanted to yell "no!" unclip myself, and run out of the exam room away from the pain I knew was coming. *God, help me! I know they need this measurement, but I'm close to freaking out right now. I know You have me. Help me trust You.* The doctor was ready to start, so I forced my attention to what he said about the test not causing much pain and tried not to throw up.

The first electric current was uncomfortable, but the next level instantly brought tears. *God, please come and take this pain from me.* Dr. Vissar reached out to put his hand on my knee. "This is painful. I sorry."

Didn't he just tell me this test wasn't painful? I wondered if he had mixed up his English or perhaps had the bizarre idea that patients needed to be told up front that it wouldn't hurt. I guessed that when we patients were jolted off the table with our pubic hair on fire, then he'd admit it was painful.

Dr. Vissar repeated the test on both the right and left sides of the clitoris and inside the anal cavity. Shaking and crying, all I could think was, *And I haven't even had the surgery yet.*

Lord, I need You. I need You, I prayed in silence.

"I would have preferred to be told the test was painful before we started," I said, wiping my tears on my sleeve. "I do better when I know ahead of time, so I can prepare my mind."

I had no idea if he understood, especially since I was talking so fast with my squeaky, tear-choked voice.

"It is good. Next test to be asleep for you," he said.

"Next test?"

I could barely breathe.

"Yes, after surgery tomorrow, we will test for clear nerve. Make sure nerve is free with this test. You will sleep when test," he said. "This test is very good. Today we know the left pudendal neuralgia is very bad. We have 11.3 on the left and 3.2 on the right. After surgery, 3–3.6 on left and right."

He smiled in an attempt to sound encouraging. Undone by the shock of what I had just endured, I could only stare into the distance.

Later I asked Dr. Bedeau why the numbers of the latency test didn't match the numbers of the same test in America. He told me the tests they performed in France were more accurate. Their results indicated my right side was normal. I wasn't shouting victory yet, but it did give me hope.

My legs wobbled as I got up from the table. I guess it's not French etiquette to help one off the examining table when you have no clothes on your lower half, even when you're about to pass out. I tried to put on my underwear without falling over. My jeans proved no easier. There—finally.

I held on to the wall and hobbled out of the exam room to greet my two faithful compatriots.

"How you doin', kiddo?" Patty asked.

My eyes filled again. "Awful," I squeaked.

When we left the building, she asked, "What did they do in there?"

Both Sheila's and Patty's mouths fell open when I described in detail what I had endured behind the closed door.

"That's barbaric," said Sheila.

"Why can't they give you some kind of numbing medication before they zap you like that?" Patty asked.

"If they gave you drugs to numb the area, it would alter the nerve response. You just have to suck it up," I said.

"Well you are through sucking it up, girl. This is going to work. You are going to be better when all this is over," Patty said, rubbing my back. "Do you want me to jog back and get the car for you?"

"No thanks, I'll crawl back." I tried to joke, since we all needed something to laugh about.

Our next stop was the hospital to meet my anesthesiologist. Sheila guided us through the red tape. On the second floor in a sparsely furnished room, a thirty-something guy in blue scrubs greeted us.

"Hi, I'm Sam, the anesthesiologist for Dr. Bedeau."

"Wow, your English is great," we said in unison.

"I'm actually from Belgium," Sam said.

After he collected his consultation fee of two hundred euros, we went over the procedures for the next day's surgery. Sam was seated with a four-inch pad of paper in front of him.

"So, tell me about your history with anesthesia. I know you've had quite a few surgeries; Dr. Bedeau forwarded me your chart notes. I am a barfer. With anesthesia, there has never been a time when I have not tossed my cookies. I've had anesthesiologists mix drug cocktails for me, claiming I'd be fine, but in the end I hurled."

"I'm pretty good at mixing cocktails that do work, so you can trust me." Sam leaned forward. "We have some drugs here that the United States doesn't have. You're going to have your first surgery without vomiting."

While Sam jotted notes on his pad, I answered. "Even though the odds are stacked against you, I like your confidence. What really allows me to trust you, though, is the part about France having drugs America doesn't have."

Sam grinned.

"So, we're good then?" he said.

"Good as it gets, I guess." I had picked my stubby nails down to the quick while pacing the room. I couldn't wait to exit.

When we left the building, Sheila said, "What do you know about that? There's an anesthesiologist named Sam right here in France."

"I don't care if his name is Quiche Lorraine. I'm just glad he spoke English and listened to me about my barfing," I said.

"Maybe this will be an easy surgery for you, Jo. I have a good feeling about it," Patty remarked.

"Well, we'll see," I said. "It could hardly be much worse than most of the others."

Patty and Sheila strolled while I shuffled back to the hotel so I could rest and pack up for my hospital stay. Most Americans strolling on that city street in the south of France were dreaming of wine and food, absorbed in the beauty surrounding them.

While some people wanted a good French wine, I wanted a fire extinguisher for my mind. Flaming arrows of fear, dread, and doubt flew around my brain and set my hope ablaze, threatening to leave only ashes.

God, help me. I know You have to be in this or I wouldn't be here. You made the heaven and the earth, and I know You have me too, I prayed, trying to convince myself, when a passage from Scripture came to mind: "I lift up my eyes to the hills. From where does my help come? My help comes from the LORD, who made heaven and earth" (Psalm 121:1–2 ESV).

Thank You for the reminder, God. I have to shift my focus to only You. I know nothing is impossible for You. If You made the heavens and the earth, You can take care of me having another surgery, even if it's five thousand miles from home.

I forced my mind to quit replaying the medical failures I'd endured; but my distress threatened to choke me anyway. I was doing my best to look to God while trying to stuff down the terror of surgery. I shuffled farther along the street and thought about hospital check-in.

In just a few hours I would be admitted.

14

Check-in Night

*The friend in my adversity I shall always cherish most. I can better
trust those who helped to relieve the gloom of my dark hours than those
who are so ready to enjoy with me the sunshine of my prosperity.*

—Ulysses S. Grant

When we returned to the hotel, one of the front desk
staff called Sheila over. She was informed that another
American patient of Dr. Bedeau's had checked in and was scheduled for surgery the same day as mine. Patty and Sheila went
to meet the woman and her husband, while I returned to our
hotel room.

I collapsed on the bed and squeezed back tears as I swallowed a handful of pain meds to dull the searing pain in my
pelvis. I watched the clock. I tried to read my Bible and pray.
Crying, I wrote a paragraph in my journal. It was ninety minutes
until check-in.

God, You are my Father, the Father of my heart, mind, and soul. Your Holy Spirit lives in me. Your Word says that You are my strength and my very present help in times of trouble. My heart's cry is that You would show Yourself mighty on my behalf. You see me. You made me and You know how weak I am. Be my strength, Lord. I don't have any of my own. I need You.

When I thumbed through previous journal entries, my eyes rested on a quote by Charles Spurgeon that I had written at the top of a page: "Believing Soul, if you are in the dark you are near the King's cellars where the well-defined wines on the racks are stored. You are in the Lord's pavilion and you may speak with Him. Thanks God, that You are always listening."

My quiet moment with God ended abruptly when Patty and Sheila burst into the hotel room.

Sheila started first. "Jo, we just found out the weirdest thing. The American patient we went to see is from Boston! Can you believe that? She lives not too far from us. How wild!"

"What an odd coincidence, right?" Patty chimed in. "Her American ob-gyn brought her to France because he had performed a surgery on her bladder after she gave birth. After the birth of the baby and the subsequent surgery, she did not heal correctly. She was diagnosed with pudendal nerve entrapment shortly after. Her doctor wanted to do whatever he could to help her regain her life."

"Now that's some serious medical care. He must be a really compassionate doctor." I was trying to engage with the story of the other patient, but my eyes kept filling with tears.

"Hey, listen, we're going to give you some space. It's time to leave soon, so Sheila and I are going to go to the lobby to read, okay?" Patty said.

I nodded and started to pack for the hospital. After packing, I tried to keep myself occupied by pacing. An hour later, I downed more pain pills and met Patty in the lobby. Because Sheila had already been assured by Dr. Bedeau that the hospital check-in was an easy process and the admitting clerk spoke some English, she decided to run to the store to get a few snack items and drinks to keep in the hospital room; she would be twenty minutes behind us. Patty hoisted my overnight bag over her shoulder, and we walked the short distance to the hospital.

The admitting clerk spoke English and directed me to my room after collecting our fee for the use of the hospital room telephone. My nurse, Terese, greeted us warmly, but she spoke almost no English. We played charades for fifteen minutes until Sheila arrived. Through Sheila, we began to understand how things would shake out. An older man with a suit and tie entered and said a few words to Terese. Her smile faded as she walked quickly out of the room with her head down. With a very heavy accent, he introduced himself as Dr. Shafir, my anesthesiologist.

"I am from Paris, and have recently joined Dr. Bedeau to help with his foreign patients," he said.

I stopped unzipping my overnight bag and a huge lump formed in my throat. My voice squeaked, "What happened to Sam? He has all my information."

"Sam shouldn't have interviewed you. I am here now." He reeked of arrogance.

Panic joined the lump in my throat. I tried to swallow it down, but it was like swallowing a loaf of bread with no water. My tongue stuck to the roof of my mouth.

"Do not worry, Madam, I will take good care of you." He leered at me, looked through my medications, and then sauntered out of the room.

"Oh, my gosh! You can feel the sleaze dripping off that guy," Patty whispered.

Sheila looked at Patty and then to me. Her eyes narrowed. "Yep, he's a little too slick for me."

"Are you kidding me? Sam I trust. This doctor gives me the creeps."

I stood there too stunned to respond.

We unpacked my things and tried to keep the conversation light.

As Patty organized my belongings into a large freestanding armoire, Sheila walked out onto the small balcony of the hospital room. A view of a modest garden in the middle of the quad-shaped hospital was shared by each room overlooking it. Sheila stepped back in and left the sliding door open. I climbed into my hospital bed while Patty and Sheila flopped onto the adjacent bed. All of us noticed something dark moving under their bed.

"It's a pigeon!" yelled Patty. "Get it out, Sheila. Hurry!"

The two of them scrambled madly to get the uncooperative bird out through the slider. After ten minutes of tactical command operations, laughter and shrieking, they cleared the room. The disheveled bird stayed put on the balcony peering in. We were laughing so hard we could hardly breathe.

"Well, clearly the metaphor of this entire trip is, 'Shoo out the pigeons and shut the door!'" Patty howled.

"I can't think of anything that wouldn't apply to," Sheila snorted.

We were sure our shrieking laughter brought back my nurse, Terese. She smiled and spoke with Sheila in French.

"She wants you to know that she is here to help you in any way you need, Jo. She loves her work but is frustrated and embarrassed that she doesn't speak any English."

"Tell her thank you, Sheila. Please let her know it's no problem that she doesn't speak English. I don't speak any French, and I don't feel bad," I joked.

I looked at Terese and smiled. I liked her. I was disappointed that she would be on duty for only three of the days I was there.

Soon after Terese returned to the nurses' station, Dr. Bedeau stopped in to welcome us. "Madam Joanne, Madam Sheila, and Madam Patty, it is good to see you. You are getting settled in? Terese is here with us a long time and a good nurse. She will be a help to you. Everything will go well. My team is ready for your surgery, and it is routine for us since we have been so many years together doing this."

"Thank you, Dr. Bedeau. Terese is very kind, and I appreciate that your team is confident my surgery will go well. I'm just wondering why Sam is not my anesthesiologist. I felt comfortable with him, and he has my history about the severe vomiting reaction I have from all anesthesia."

He smiled but did not understand my concern. "Dr. Shafir is coming from Paris to join our team. He has many years of experience. He will take care of you. Sam is not working with international patients." With that, he nodded and turned down the hall. My throat lump was back.

Sheila planned to return to the hotel while Patty stayed with me overnight in the hospital. Before she left, she showed Patty how to work the telephone with its several codes to enter at different prompts to make a call. All the prompts were in French, making it difficult for us. The day before, we had tried to purchase a cell phone in a local shop, but there were no phone cards available, and local phones required a one-year contract. Since we didn't have international cell phone coverage, the hospital phone was our only option for outside calls.

Patty and I settled in for the night. Both of us picked our cuticles while I wondered aloud if I had made a mistake in coming here.

"I'm sure it'll be fine," she said.

"Yeah, what choices were left anyway?" I sighed.

"Bev will be here soon, and you know she always makes things better. Don't worry," Patty said.

A nurse came in and explained with hand motions and nods that I was to use the topical antibiotic and shave.

"You, yes?" she said.

"Oui," I answered, getting out of bed to take the used razor and bottle of cleaning solution she handed me.

I entered the shower and began the formidable task in front of me. "Does she mean all of it?" Patty yelled over the shower noise.

"Bald," I yelled back. "This razor won't cut one hair, and I think fourteen other patients have used this before me."

"Gross," Patty yelled back. "I'll get yours from your overnight bag."

Presented with my new, pink Lady Daisy Teflon-coated wonder, I finished the job in ten minutes. "I would have been in there for four days trying to use that other razor."

"You couldn't have cut yourself, though," Patty said with a snicker.

We laughed about some other things and tried not to think about what the morning would bring. Patty turned out the light and quiet descended.

"Thanks for being here and doing all this for me, Patty," I said in the dark.

"Are you kidding? I wouldn't miss this for anything! Think of the mileage we're going to get from all the stories!"

I couldn't spin any more threads in my web of worry so I tried to pray and fall asleep.

※

The morning rode in like a Harley with fear strapped in the sidecar. Sheila came early to the hospital in case translation was needed, and I uttered a continual stream of prayer to God to help keep me from hyperventilating. A burly medical orderly came to get me for surgery prep while Patty headed to the airport to get our sister Bev.

The surgical prep nurse flitted around my gurney and tried to engage me in conversation. My limited language skills were obvious from the start.

She said, "Le Francais?"

I said, "No."

"Italian?"

"No."

"German?"

"No."

She spoke so many languages; I waited for her to ask me if I spoke Icelandic. Finally she said, "Espanol?"

I said, "*Si, poquisimo.*" (Very little.)

I began to sweat, remembering just how *poquisimo* Spanish I could speak. Much to my surprise, five years of junior high and high school Spanish paid off, and I understood most of what she asked me. Her eyes shone above her surgical mask. I could tell she was smiling underneath it. She told me that my orange toenail polish was the most beautiful color and decided that with the gold foil Mylar sheet she had draped over me I looked like a delicious piece of white chocolate. Either that or she was telling me something about my upcoming surgery.

I decided to think about being a piece of white chocolate under gold wrapping—it was just easier that way.

15

Death to Life

*I will remember that there is art to medicine as well as
science, and that warmth, sympathy, and understanding
may outweigh the surgeon's knife or the chemist's drug.*

—Louis Lasagna, Modern Hippocratic Oath, 1964

I remember clearly that I was slipping away—as if I were disappearing. The surgery was over, and I was in my hospital room. I kept pleading for help with the pain that was ripping through my body. Yet I knew that all the pain medicine in the world wouldn't make any difference. With each heartbeat, I felt another warm gush of blood run down my backside. I could hear my sisters talking. Patty's shoes made a whooshing sound on the floor. I could tell she was pacing.

Bev touched my arm. "Look at her color, Patty. She looks gray."

The sound of Patty's footsteps came closer. "She feels really warm."

With my eyes still shut, I felt Bev lean in closer to my face. "Do you know what's wrong?" she asked me.

I could barely whisper an answer. "I think I'm bleeding to death."

They pushed the nurse call button. I heard two young French nurses step into my room. Before forcing my eyes open, I sensed their hostility and smelled the cigarette smoke on their uniforms. We had experienced their scorn days earlier when I first checked into the hospital. Sheila told us, based on her interactions with different hospital employees, that many on the nursing staff considered Americans to be high-maintenance patients. Now the nurses looked primed for battle. None of us needed to understand French to decipher the contemptuous look on their faces or the arms folded over their chests.

Standing on both sides of my bed, my sisters began to speak at once: "Feel her head . . . look at her color . . . something is wrong."

One nurse stayed at the doorway, while the other, a blond, stepped toward my bed. Although she had claimed not to speak any English, she clearly understood what they were trying to say.

I watched as she pulled down the bedclothes and looked at the surgical pad between my legs. The stench of stale cigarette smoke made me gag. "Normale," she said, with a shrug of her shoulders and a dismissive wave. The disdainful look on her face caused a wave of fear to come over me. She showed Patty and Bev the examined area and then jerked the sheet back up.

When the nurse turned and began to walk toward the door, Patty followed after her. "Normal? She isn't normal at all. Look at her color. Can't you see that something is wrong? She needs the doctor!" Patty, inches from the nurse's face, breathed hard. "She's in so much pain. Help her!"

"Je suis tres mal," said Bev, repeating the words Sheila had taught us to say if I needed to report I was in very bad pain. The words sent Patty into tears.

Bev's eyes also filled. In another attempt to shake the nurses into action, she begged, "Please, call Dr. Bedeau!"

The blonde nurse joined her colleague at the doorway. She shook her head and scowled. "No Bedeau." Then they turned and walked down the hall chattering, as casually as if they were discussing their next smoke break.

With each passing second, I was more certain that I would not survive. I could not endure this pain any longer. I had prayed to God continually while on this trip, but I was entering a place where I could not utter another appeal. Pain wracked me to my core and consumed me. I could not escape. I sensed a depth to this suffering that felt final. The agony of it overrode the pain that I had endured day in and day out for the last six years. Even through other horrific surgeries, I had never known pain like this.

With my eyes closed, I listened to my sisters' voices. Patty's hinted of hysteria. "They don't know her. They don't know her, Bev. If she says she's bleeding and in agony, then it is serious. They don't know how much pain she can take. She's in trouble. We've got to get Sheila over here."

I heard someone grab the telephone and start punching keys.

"This stupid phone," Bev yelled. "The codes they gave us to dial out of the hospital don't work!"

"That phone has never worked for anyone but Sheila." Patty's voice was filled with fury.

The phone rang in Bev's hand; it was our father calling from Indiana. "It's not looking good, Dad. Something is really wrong. We have to call you back."

I opened my eyes in time to see Patty grab the phone out of Bev's hand.

"Great! Anyone can call us from across the world, but we can't call the hotel one mile away." She frantically punched in the codes over and over again—still nothing—not even a dial tone. Disgusted, she threw the phone on the bed where Bev sat and resumed pacing at a faster speed.

"I'm going to sprint back to the hotel and get Sheila," Patty said.

"I don't think you can get back fast enough, Patty."

Patty suddenly stopped and turned to stare at Bev. "What are you saying?"

Bev was now standing beside me crying. She reached her hand out to smooth my hair. "We need the doctor."

With her hand touching my head, I felt the heaviness of my eyelids again. No effort on my part could hold them open. Pain engulfed me.

Suddenly Sheila burst into the room. "I ran all the way here! I knew something was wrong! I knew it. I just kept hearing, 'Get over there. Get over there.'"

Sentence after sentence poured from her mouth. "I've been throwing up all morning from food poisoning or something, but I couldn't shake this voice telling me to get here as fast as I could. I ran by those men at the corner who ask about Jo every day, and I yelled for them to pray!"

Sheila ran to me and began stroking my hair. "Don't worry, Jo. We'll get help."

Patty reached over and grabbed Sheila's shoulder. "She's terrible, Sheila! She told us she's bleeding!"

Sheila ran out the door saying, "Don't worry. I am calling Dr. Bedeau on his cell right now." We heard her screaming in French for the nurses in the hallway.

I could smell the nurses entering my room again with Sheila and then Sheila's voice escalating rapid-fire French on her cell phone. I heard the shouting and the crying, but my eyes remained shut.

Sheila rushed to my bedside once more. "Dr. Bedeau is on his way down from surgery, Jo. Hang on."

I heard the loud clicking of Dr. Shafir's shoes before I heard his voice.

"I am here to help. What is causing all the problem here?"

"Why don't you do something for her?" Patty yelled.

"You are upsetting your sister," he replied.

"Upsetting my sister? She's in agony, you idiot, and no one is doing anything about it!"

The nurses and anesthesiologist fired words to each other in French.

Sheila's voice was close to my head. "They think you and Patty are upsetting Joanne and that's why she's complaining."

"This is insane," Bev said.

Patty dissolved into frustrated sobs, and I heard the clicking of the anesthesiologist's shoes leave the room. I felt my bed suddenly wheeled into the hall after him. I could hear Dr. Bedeau speaking directly over my head as he leaned in close to my face, "Joanne, what are you so afraid of?"

His question completely confused me, and I tried to force my eyes open, hoping he would see my torment. My response was almost inaudible. "I'm not afraid of anything. I'm just in so much pain. Please help me."

His hand patted my shoulder. "Okay, okay. We will take care."

He began barking orders into the crowded hallway as my bed was wheeled toward the elevator that went up to the surgical suites.

Dr. Bedeau's words didn't comfort me. In my spirit I knew that by the time I got upstairs it would be too late.

Once through the surgical doors, the medical team wouldn't allow my sisters or Sheila to enter. I was certain I wouldn't see them again. Abruptly, a bizarre thought flooded my head. *How odd this will be, Lord, to die in a place where almost no one understands English.*

Back inside the surgical prep area, the anesthesiologist, Dr. Shafir, rushed to my bedside. "What is wrong, Joanna?"

I couldn't answer. He couldn't even get my name right.

He started shouting. I forced my eyes open a slit to see two male nurses ready to jab huge needles into my arms and legs to get a port into my body to administer anesthesia. Over and over they jabbed and failed. I didn't recognize the sounds coming from my mouth. I screamed like a wild animal each time they jammed in another needle. I felt I was being tortured to death. They couldn't have had any comprehension of the level of pain they were inflicting. I could no longer feel my heart beating, but a flow of warm blood continued to gush from my vagina. *Why doesn't anyone turn me over and check? Why don't they see that I am bleeding to death?*

I felt Dr. Shafir's hot breath on my face. "Joanna, we will put you on your side. Open your eyes!"

I could not comprehend why I needed to open them. Holding my eyes open even a slit increased my torment. Through the narrow opening, I saw perspiration running down the doctor's face.

"We must get the needle in your back. We cannot get it in your arms and legs!"

I would learn later that all my veins had collapsed; my spine offered their last hope to administer general anesthesia. The two male nurses and Dr. Shafir began to turn me on my side.

Agony ripped through my body as if I were being sliced apart with knives. In my trauma, I cried out to God: *Take me from this pain. Please, God, please. I can't hang on. Take me from here. Help me. Please, let me go. Let me go!* I was screaming with an inaudible voice.

Just then, amid the most excruciating pain I had ever experienced, the torment lifted. For the first time in six years, I felt no pain. Instead, weightlessness and peace enveloped me. In that moment, I was transported by a blinding bright light that drew me up to the ceiling. From my high vantage point, I viewed the chaotic scene below with surprising detachment. I felt no emotion or connection to my body or the activity around it.

The people filling the room were scrambling and yelling. I couldn't understand their language, but I watched their anguished, panic-stricken faces as they tried to revive my lifeless body. It lay there quietly, in a crumpled heap on the gurney. I could see that they had managed to turn it on its side. I saw that I had bled all the way through the thick hospital mattress and onto the floor. I saw Dr. Shafir yell at Phillipe, the head nurse, to place my body on the top bed sheet so that the others would not see the amount of blood that had drained out of it.

Despite the adrenaline-pumping activity in the room, I had one calming thought—*I am never going back to that pain. I am finally free!*

I looked away from the bedlam below to focus on the serenity that surrounded me, wrapping itself around me like a protective blanket.

Before I heard Him, I felt the overwhelming presence of God eclipse the room. A thunderous voice overwhelmed me. "I have seen your suffering, child, and I know full well your pain."

This voice was vast and consuming, filling every corner of

the room and every part of me. Its gentleness soaked into every part of my being. As I listened, I felt the voice—His voice—express a love so deep, the same love that had woven me together in my innermost places. I knew I was in the presence of my Creator and Lord.

"You may come with Me now or you may stay, for there is much work for you to do. The prayers of the saints have given you a choice."

I was incapable of making sense of what I heard. I struggled as a wave of reactions washed over me. He is so boundless that, in contrast, I was acutely aware of my insignificance. I was overwhelmed with awe of Him and humbled in His presence. I wanted to duck—to fold myself into something smaller in His presence—but I realized I had no physical body to duck with. There are no words to adequately describe an encounter with the holy, living God.

I uttered a barely intelligible, "What?"

God spoke again, "The prayers of the saints have given you a choice."

What was He saying? There was a choice? I had a choice?

I glanced down to watch the escalating mayhem below me. The frantic activity centered around my unresponsive body. More people entered the scene. Sweat poured down the faces of Phillipe and Dr. Shafir. I knew my choice. Without uttering a word, I knew my decision. Of course, I would go with Him.

In the next instant, I saw my son's face before me, displayed not as on a screen or projected as a holographic image but vivid and lifelike; I felt I could almost reach out and touch Kian's face. Behind him, I could see my husband. When I saw them, I knew instinctively that they were some of the work the Lord had referred to when He first spoke. My deepest desire was to be freed from the torture of my earthly body, but in that split second I made an unspoken decision.

"It is as you wish, child," He said, affirming my decision. "You must understand that a force of great magnitude will come against you that will cause you pain as you have never known before."

He can't mean that, I thought. *Please, not more pain.*

His voice covered me again. "This pain will come as you meet your body. It will go quickly, and you will again know the pain you lie in at this moment. There is purpose in your suffering, child, and pain will be a part of you—sometimes fierce, unrelenting pain. Remember My promises. Do not fear, My child, for I will never leave you. I will be with you minute by minute."

The trailing words *minute by minute* were still ringing in my mind as the force of a freight train struck me. *Slam!* The pain was beyond anything I had known. Yet, it was different from the pain I had left behind. I had no breath. Everything about me felt shattered, like shards of glass embedded throughout my body. *Minute by minute.*

The shattering pain evaporated within seconds, and I felt again the familiar searing agony that had caused me to cry out for the end of my life. I screamed aloud as the huge needle was jammed into my spinal canal. And then there came a warm flood of relief.

The head nurse, Phillipe, took my hand as he leaned over my face with tears streaming down his cheeks. "I'm so sorry, Madam. I'm so sorry."

I was wheeled into the operating room and fell into unconsciousness.

Hours later, back in my hospital room, I awoke in pain; the

epidural had been removed. God's words echoed inside my mind: *More pain . . . I will never leave you . . . minute by minute.*

My sisters and Sheila surrounded me. Bev moved closer and touched my hand. "We are so glad to see you."

"We didn't think we were going to see you again, kiddo," Sheila said, kissing my forehead.

Patty paced the room then came over again to smooth my hair. Her gentle touch seemed at odds with her next comment. "We have to get you out of here. They don't know what they're doing at this hospital."

I could think only of the words *minute by minute.* Although God had warned me of more pain, I could not imagine anything worse than what I had just been through. I asked Bev to get the pain meds I had brought from home out of the drawer beside my bed. Even though my sisters begged for another epidural, pleas for greater pain control went unheeded by Dr. Shafir. Without further consideration, he told us that I didn't need that much medication to control my pain level.

I slept most of the day while Bev investigated why lab reports were not available. As I drifted in and out of consciousness, I heard: "She had to have lost a ton of blood" and "Where are her labs?"

Bev, a knowledgeable medical technologist, was perplexed at the cavalier way my case was being treated by the anesthesiologist. Patty was enraged. Sheila called the doctor's office for answers. She heard only more of the same—the anesthesiologist was in charge of my pain control.

Every time I awakened, I asked for more pain meds. My faithful companions dipped into my own bottles time and again. Minutes later I would be asleep. Bev had opted to stay the night with me while Patty and Sheila got away on a day-trip to the coast in an attempt to regain their sanity.

At dusk I awoke to find Philippe by my bedside. He took my hand and apologized to me again for what had happened earlier. In fractured English he tried to explain what had gone wrong. Before he finished his first sentence, Dr. Shafir burst through the door and cast Philippe a contemptuous look. Philippe's eyes bored into mine as if to say, "You understand what is really happening here, right?" With a nod, he hurried out the door. Bev watched with her mouth agape.

Dr. Shafir's voice broke the uncomfortable silence. "You are feeling much better now—yes, Joanna?"

Shifting my head to the left, I was able to stare directly at his face. This man had the power to ease my constant suffering, yet he didn't concern himself with the matter at all. I repeated the words I was so tired of saying: "I'm still in too much pain."

"I will take care, no worry. Your sisters make you worry," he said.

I was glad that Patty and Sheila weren't there to hear his words.

Bev stood from her seated position on the end of my bed and turned to face the anesthesiologist. "Why won't you give her an epidural so she can have a break from this pain?"

"She will be better. No more epidural now."

Bev and I sighed together as Dr. Shafir walked to the door. Looking back over his shoulder he announced, "I will be back."

His words hung in the air and sent a chill through me. I began to cry again as I listened to the clicking sound of his polished wing-tips growing fainter down the hall.

I sighed. "Thank you for coming, Bev."

"Oh, you silly girl, I wouldn't be anywhere else."

I then began to tell her what had happened to me in the operating room. Her jaw fell open, and tears sprang to her eyes. "Oh, my gosh! Oh, my gosh! That is unreal."

I was too tired to speak anymore and drifted back to sleep. "Minute by minute" played over and over in my mind.

How much longer must I endure this, God?

16

A New Torture

No one is useless in this world who lightens the burdens of another.

—CHARLES DICKENS

In the middle of the night I awoke with leg cramps. Not wanting to awaken Bev, I tried shaking them lightly. The cramping increased to burning. Hot fire traveled down my thighs into my calf muscles.

I touched the tops of my thighs and instead felt solid granite—my muscles were in full spasm. I cried out for Bev, and she rang for the nurse. Speaking no English, the responding nurse showed no sympathy for my plight. She shrugged her shoulders and walked out.

"We're on our own," Bev said with a weary sigh. "I'll rub them."

She began rubbing them gently, and immediately my legs jumped up and down in spastic jerks. Joining the spasms was the strange sensation of my legs being seared with a hot poker.

"Pound them, Bev," I urged.

"You have to try and keep still as I pound," she said as she flailed her fists into my rock-hard thighs. "They're like steel. This is bizarre! Didn't anyone say anything about this side effect from the surgery? Maybe they touched a nerve and set this whole thing off." She gasped out the words between blows.

While Bev hammered on my legs for more than an hour, I yelled through clenched teeth, "They need to be tied really tight with something like a tourniquet. Maybe that will help somehow." I involuntarily flexed and curled my feet in reaction to the cramps.

Bev ran around the room looking for T-shirts, towels, or anything else she could tie around my thighs and calves. I bemoaned the fact, yet again, that hospitals under socialized medicine, did not provide basic conveniences, including towels.

Bev found two cotton jersey pajama tops and a T-shirt in the suitcase I had brought to the hospital. She tied them tightly around each leg. The searing pain shifted to a pulsating ache.

"Please go back to sleep, Bev. I'll be okay," I said. She leaned against the mattress with both hands and exhaled in exhaustion.

"I will if you promise to wake me if it gets out of control again," she said as she reluctantly climbed back into the bed next to mine.

"I will. I promise." The sounds of her deep breathing were all I heard in response.

I pulled my CD player off the bedside table and put on the headphones. *Please God, please God, please God—help me get through this,* I begged.

Even with the tight wraps, the cramps were full blown again within an hour. I cried and prayed, prayed and cried. With my IV in one wrist and the oxygen sensor attached to my other hand, I whaled on my legs the best I could. I did not want to awaken my weary sister again.

I tried to retie the shirts, but I didn't have the strength to manage. Desperate to stop the spasms, I was determined to go to the open shower five feet away. I reasoned that the contractions might go away if I put my legs in hot water. The thought of the relief that would come if I ran scalding water on my legs was the only thing I could focus on.

I yanked off the tourniquets and pulled my urinary catheter bag up from the hook under my bed. Since the surgery, I was under orders to not move at all; but none of that mattered to me now. Slowly, I tried to sit up and scoot off the bed. My heart lurched as I fell forward, nearly off the bed. My head spun and sickened me.

Shaking, nauseous, carrying the urine bag, and pushing the IV pole, I inched my way into the bathroom shower stall, which fortunately had no lip to step over or curtain to pull. With trembling hands, I knotted my nightshirt around my waist and reached to hold on to a safety bar as I waited for the water to get hot. The scalding water countered the searing in my muscles, and sweet relief began to flood over me. I caught my breath and looked up through the steamy shower stall.

Why, God? Why does it have to be so hard?

Running water was my only reply. When the hot water ran cold, I tried to dry off my legs. They buckled beneath me and I caught myself on the safety bar. Wobbling toward the bed, I gave the IV pole one last push, hung the urine bag, and collapsed. It had taken me nearly twenty minutes to make it back the five feet to my bed.

Bev never woke during the ordeal. The numbers on my watch glowed 4:30. The hellish night ended with the five o'clock vitals check by the next shift of nurses. All major convulsions in my legs ceased with the rising of the sun. My thigh muscles remained as solid as petrified wood, but the pain was now tolerable.

The words of the Lord soothed my thoughts again: *I will never leave you.* I held on to them as my lifeline. I couldn't imagine what else could happen to test my faith and trust in Him.

The next morning, Patty and Sheila recounted their day on the coast in Marseilles.

"We actually drove along the coast of Marseilles, like a real vacation!" Patty said. "It's amazing how your perspective can change when you get out of this hospital."

"We took a bunch of pictures so we'll be able to show you what you missed." Sheila chimed in.

Bev looked over at me and smiled. "We're glad you both got out. You needed it. And, don't you worry, Jo. We'll come back another time, when you are free from all this, and see the France you've missed."

Their stories lifted some of the heaviness that had settled in my room and brought the gift of laughter. The two of them left again a few hours later to sort out lodging in another hotel for my eventual release from the hospital. Our original hotel room had accommodations for three and we would need four beds when I was released.

I drifted to sleep again, but when I woke I felt a familiar sensation. "Hey, Bev?"

"What's up?" she asked as she looked up from her book.

"That same pain that I had with the start of the hemorrhaging feels like it's coming back." I started to cry.

A look of horror crossed her face. "Are you sure it feels the same?"

"I could feel fear rising even along my hairline. "It feels the same, but I don't feel any gushing of blood."

"You tell me what you need, okay?"

"Can you hand me more pain pills? I'm going back to sleep and see if it's gone when I wake up."

I had been asleep for an hour when Dr. Bedeau came by to see me with his five-year-old son. The boy looked like an angel with his blond, curly hair and big blue eyes that peered at me from behind his tall father's legs. I cried, thinking of my own son so close to his age. I recalled the picture God had given me and wondered how I would ever make it home to my family.

Each time the child would say "Papa" with his French accent, my eyes would well up with unbidden tears.

Dr. Bedeau took a seat on the end of my bed and turned to face me with a hopeful smile.

"How are you today, Joanne?"

"My pain is becoming more intense again. It feels as if the same pain from the bleeding is coming back." I was so weary of those words and frightened by what I thought was happening to me again.

He stood and pulled down the sheet to check my lower abdomen.

"I will call for Dr. Shafir before I leave, and he will come."

"Please ask him to give me better pain control, Dr. Bedeau. I'm in so much pain. Why doesn't he understand?"

A worried look flashed across his face that he quickly covered with a reassuring smile.

"He is new to our group but very great—from a big hospital in Paris. I am trusting in his experience to help my patients with pain. I hope he is doing the best for you."

At that I closed my eyes in resignation to rest and pray.

I know I had the chance to go with you, God. I have no right to complain. You warned me. You told me it wasn't going to be easy. But I never dreamed it would be this hard.

The only thing I heard was conversation between Bev and the doctor as I closed my eyes and drifted in and out of sleep.

Dr. Bedeau spoke to Bev at great length. Each time I awoke I heard her ask many questions about my recovery, particularly about the night cramps.

"I have not heard of any patient having these leg cramps. Perhaps the loss of blood has caused Joanne to require more magnesium. I will prescribe for her to have magnesium each night."

"That would be helpful, thank you. She has suffered for so long."

"Yes, it is unfortunate the suffering of American patients. So different, the diagnosis time, from our ways in France."

In detail he compared for Bev the French versus United States approach to pudendal nerve entrapment. "Here it is treated as a common disorder and properly diagnosed within six months of onset. In America, the patient suffers, on average, ten unnecessary surgeries before finally being properly diagnosed.

"As you know, many patients have suffered more than ten years with this disorder and did not receive a proper diagnosis until they were tested through your sister's doctor in San Francisco. We hope for the best for Joanne, but she has had this condition much too long for us to be certain that she will not have some pain for the rest of her life."

I heard the sadness in his voice as he continued. "I hope this will not be the case, but we must wait possibly two years before we see how much decrease in pain she will have. The nerve often takes a very long time to show improvement."

I finally opened my eyes and told him that the pain was

becoming very sharp. He came over to my side and checked the pad between my legs while his son went down the hall with a nurse who had come to collect him.

I pleaded silently. *Please, God, not again.*

"You have been through much trauma, Joanne. I will call Dr. Shafir at his hotel now and have him come right away to help you with your pain. There may be some small hematoma from the bleeding, which can cause much pain. We will see tomorrow if you have improvement. Please have Sheila call my cell phone, if you are still having much trouble."

When Dr. Bedeau prepared to leave, Bev stood. "Do you have her blood panel after the second surgery?"

He looked perplexed. "We did not take blood after that repair. She had a rupture of the left inferior gluteal artery, which is most uncommon. It has happened only twice before in the ten years since we have been doing the nerve decompression. We were able to close it quickly, so no problem. If Joanne continues to have pain, we will have an ultrasound done for her."

He patted my leg and looked at me with concern. "I am sorry this happened to you."

After the doctor left, Bev returned to the end of my bed. She took my feet in her hands and lightly rubbed the tops. "It's weird that he's so casual about all of this. Why didn't Dr. Bedeau say anything about the amount of blood loss? How are we to know if you need a transfusion?"

"The whole thing is bizarre. Why can't he get involved in my pain control? Shafir doesn't know how to manage pain. I'm totally helpless in the hands of that guy, the great self-professed pain eliminator." I began to sob.

"He's a sadist."

With the pain increasing with each passing second, I again

felt grateful I had brought so much medication with me to France. Remembering what God said, I chose to believe it wasn't another bleed-out. But I couldn't understand why the pain continued to escalate.

As if on cue, Dr. Shafir rolled in. He said he would allow the nurses to give me some pain pills to get me through the night, but refused my request for an epidural. With his orders in place, he was out of the room in less than three minutes. So much for my hope of effective pain control.

Bev came over to rub my arm. "I wouldn't be surprised if you have some pretty large hematomas. If you lost that much blood since they closed the bleed, there might be some internal coagulation." She sighed. "I'm so sorry you're suffering like this, Jo. I don't know how you keep fighting."

Patty and Sheila returned to the hospital with plans for Patty to stay with me overnight. I could see that the stress they were enduring had etched hard lines into their faces. Patty had been sitting on the other bed, ready to brave the night with me, when suddenly, she tucked herself into a ball and began sobbing. Her expression was raw as she described her overwhelming fear that something else would go wrong. "That stupid phone. What if I can't get you guys?" she cried in desperation.

Watching Patty break down caused me to weep. I couldn't bear watching the strain that all of this had put on those I loved. I prayed silently that Patty would allow Sheila and Bev to talk her into going back to the hotel for some much-needed rest.

As if on cue, Sheila and Bev both jumped in. "Patty, stop. Don't worry. You've done enough for one day. One of us will stay the night."

Eventually, it was collectively decided that Sheila would stay because she was in the best position to help, given her command of the language. Exhausted, Bev and Patty headed back to the hotel.

Another night with cramps from hell slammed into my legs. Sheila pounded and tied tourniquet-like wraps just as Bev had the night before. The magnesium did nothing to relieve the pain. Between spasms, Sheila prayed over me.

When I shared a bit of what had happened with God in the operating room, we cried together. Until that moment, I had not known we shared such a strong faith in Christ. I had always been careful to keep my intimate relationship with God out of conversation as much as possible out of respect for my sister Patty's position as a nonbeliever. Because she and Sheila shared such a close friendship, I figured Sheila shared the same view of God that Patty had.

I was so grateful for the support of my sisters and Sheila through this journey that I certainly didn't want to offend anyone concerning matters of faith. The discovery of Sheila's faith and her praying over me was a huge comfort.

In the middle of the night, a nurse came in to check my vitals, and Sheila questioned her about the leg cramps. The nurse told her that she had seen it many times after patients had undergone this surgery. She told Sheila to run towels under hot, hot water and place them all over my legs.

When the nurse left the room, Sheila explained that she had asked the nurse why Dr. Bedeau was not aware of the cramping as a surgical side effect. The nurse apparently had little interest in the round of questions and only said she didn't know. We were dumbfounded.

Sheila provided a continuous stream of hot towels through the night.

"I'm so sorry, Sheila."

"Jo, I don't know how you can keep enduring all this. If hot towels provide you some relief, I will keep doing this for days." With that encouragement, I was finally able to fall asleep.

When Bev and Patty arrived in the morning, they were told to wait outside while my vitals were checked and I was cleaned up. I needed a bath, and hospital rules said only the attending nurse could be in the room during bathtime. Everyone would have to wait outside.

I insisted my companions take the opportunity to leave and do something fun. Patty decided they would go shopping for party stuff, as the next day, April 25, was my forty-fourth birthday. My pain continued to worsen throughout the day. When my incredible support team returned late that afternoon, laden with packages, they found me crying again from the pain. Sheila called Dr. Bedeau and an ultrasound was ordered. Unfortunately, he explained, it would have to wait until the next morning as the tech had gone home for the day.

Another night of agony ensued, with Bev by my side this time. The leg cramps had diminished, but I now suffered increasing pain across my pelvis.

It was nearly dawn, but Bev was awake.

"I feel like I have to pee really bad, but I can't."

She reached under the bed and checked my urine bag; it was nearly empty. "That's weird. With all the saline you've been given it should be almost full by now."

"Bev, help me. I can't go through this again. I keep trying to ignore the pain but it cuts through all the medication. Something is really wrong, and I don't think I have it in me to keep fighting."

"Sheila and Patty will be here at 7:30, and we're going to get you an ultrasound." She crossed the room and hugged me.

17

For the Third Time

*We don't even know how strong we are until we are forced
to bring that hidden strength forward. In times of tragedy,
of war, of necessity, people do amazing things. The human
capacity for survival and renewal is awesome.*

—ISABEL ALLENDE, AUTHOR

The next day, as I lay on a hard gurney in the hallway outside
the sonogram lab, I sobbed without restraint. The pain was
unbearable. *I am petrified, Lord.*

Inside the lab, the light touch of the ultrasound wand moving
across my abdomen caused me to shriek in pain. The sonogram
revealed three massive hematomas on top of my bladder, hip-
bones, and stomach. The technician winced at the sight of the
masses on her screen. She spoke no English but shook her head
back and forth.

"*Je suis tres mal*," I said, choking back sobs. The technician nodded with compassion in her eyes.

Wheeled back to my room, I waited for the call from Dr. Bedeau. I was too overwrought with pain to speak to him when he called Shelia's cell phone. After their brief exchange, Sheila relayed the message.

"Jo, Dr. Bedeau called instead of coming down because he's scrubbing for surgery right now. They have to take you into surgery again. He said the largest blood mass is covering your bladder so no urine is able to pass. Because your bladder is full and being crushed under the weight of the hematoma, you could sustain severe and permanent injury to your bladder. He said you are in real danger, and they are coming to get you now." Sheila was crying.

In shock, I couldn't respond. The pain was so enormous it swallowed me. I could not bear to open my eyes. Every breath was agony.

Oh, God. I made a mistake. I can't do this. You think I'm stronger than I am. I can't . . . I can't . . . please, oh, please, God . . . Help me!

My mind raced—back and forth, up and down, across, frantic and insane.

I need to die. I need to die. Let me go. I need to be out of this body. Please, God.

In all my anguish, I couldn't recall the words God had spoken to me earlier. I was frenzied with pain and panic. I would once again be in the hands of Dr. Shafir in the surgical suite. How could I endure this horror again?

The familiar figure of the orderly filled the doorway. He looked at me and shook his head. His eyes darted to Sheila, and he asked her something in French. She nodded and began to cry harder, explaining that not only was I to have surgery again, but also that it was my birthday.

For the third time in five days this orderly had come to wheel me to surgery. His kind brown eyes spilled over, dropping tears onto the sheet as he bent and cupped my cheek in his enormous mitt of a hand. He spoke softly in French to me all the way down the hall. Once inside the elevator, he began singing over me.

Tears ran down the sides of my head, as my eyes remained closed. Dread, panic, and agony suffocated me. Why had I chosen to stay? All my life I had an unrelenting resolve to complete whatever I set my mind to. I had a will of iron. Where was it now? Void of any will whatsoever, I wanted to be free from pain. That was all. I no longer cared what that meant.

Wheeled into the surgical suite once more, I began to scream out in a voice I did not recognize as my own. Pain overwhelmed me. Dr. Shafir ran forward as my bed was wheeled into the operating room. "Joanna, Joanna, what is wrong?"

I opened my eyes with the last bit of strength I had. I could not hold back my feelings for this man and for the pain I had experienced by his hands. His job was to prevent me from undergoing this agony, but he had allowed me to suffer. He was either incompetent or sadistic, and I had already formed my opinion.

"I am in so much pain! Help me!" I was screaming as wave after wave of excruciating pain washed over me. Sweat poured down my face and chest.

Dr. Shafir looked away. "Okay, okay. I fix it, I fix it." He ran across the room and grabbed what looked to be an old-fashioned, black medical bag. He rummaged through the contents and drew out a hypodermic needle, much larger than the one used for my last epidural.

I was rolled onto my side by two nurses, while Dr. Shafir

jabbed me in the spine with the enormous needle. Finally, I felt the pain begin to melt away in the slow creep of anesthetic. An IV was started, and I was ready for surgery—again.

Back in my room, still drowsy from the surgery, I heard Sheila, Bev, and Patty in a heated conversation with Dr. Shafir. Dr. Shafir was informing them that he would take out the epidural when I awoke. Hoping to outmaneuver the man, Sheila had paged Dr. Bedeau.

The words about the epidural being removed seeped into my drugged brain and jolted me awake. "*No!* Please, I am begging you. Please let me have a few days of pain control. I can't do this anymore. What kind of person are you? Please . . ." The phone rang as my voice trailed off.

"Dr. Bedeau, I'm so glad you called. Dr. Shafir is in Joanne's room right now. He wants to remove the epidural already. She can't take any more pain. She needs sleep and rest. Please, we need you to intervene." Sheila handed the phone to Dr. Shafir.

After hanging up and handing the phone back, Dr. Shafir sniffed hard and narrowed his eyes at me.

"Dr. Bedeau says to leave in. I will leave, but for three days only." He turned and left the room.

"Oh, thank God," Bev said.

"He's a barbarian—a sadist!" Patty replied.

I agreed with both comments, but I could only cry in response. This would be my first break from the unremitting pain that I had been living with for the past five days.

Patty had brought me a bouquet of purple, yellow, and red flowers. Earlier in the day, she put posters of the French countryside on the walls to brighten my room. The girls had bought me birthday gifts wrapped in butcher paper with red ribbons. I lay still and watched as they opened my presents. Patty unwrapped a beautiful French platter with the images of three women—a platter they had discovered in a small French shop just days before.

"It's the three sisters," they all said together.

Tears spilled from my eyes again. I loved it, and I loved these three women. Two of them I had loved all of my life, and Sheila I loved as the angel sent by God to help me through these desperate hours.

⧣⧤

Late in the afternoon on the second post-op day of my third surgery, Dr. Shafir came into my room unexpectedly.

"I am coming here to take out epidural," he announced.

"Wait a minute!" Bev said. "She is supposed to have this in for a total of three days so she can sleep and rest. Dr. Bedeau's orders."

"Bev, what is he doing?"

I looked at him. "Dr. Shafir, I am in too much pain for you to take this out. Please don't. I need one more day."

"No. Better to come out now." He pulled out the catheter for the medication and took the dosage meter with him. That was it.

How much more of this, God? Why did you let me live?

When Patty and Sheila arrived, a call to Dr. Bedeau yielded the same response we had gotten from Dr. Shafir.

"This is unreal. Dr. Bedeau says that Dr. Shafir was brought in because he is the expert in pain management, and Dr. Bedeau is relying on his good judgment to do what is best for you. He says you will go to the hotel in a few more days, and you will be okay."

Bev and Patty couldn't believe what they heard. "Released?"

"In a few days?"

"Have they ever checked your hemoglobin levels? We still don't know the extent of your blood loss. This is crazy!"

"We need to get her back to a hospital in the States, Bev. Let's just go with it so we can get her home." Patty started organizing items around the room as if we were leaving that minute.

How I wished that were possible. How I longed to be home in my own bed with a compassionate doctor who would help me find some relief. Any pain control was better than what I had here. In preparation for the anticipated increase in pain as the epidural wore off, Patty and Bev got my pain pills from the drawer next to my bed.

Late that afternoon, the girls went for a walk around the block. The stress had gotten to everyone. While they were out, I noticed a blond woman smoking a cigarette on the balcony that stretched the length of the building outside my room. She turned and rapped on the glass and then stuck her head through the partially opened door. "Hey, I'm Jenna. I met your sisters. Weird thing that your sister and I both live in Massachusetts, huh?"

She looked about my age, and I motioned for her to come in. She limped in slowly, with a grimace on her face and holding onto her lower abdomen.

"How's it going with you?" I asked.

"It sucks, but I'm better than you." She flopped onto the other bed. "I heard you've had a rough go of it."

"What is up with this lack of pain control?" I asked.

Jenna rolled over toward me. "I brought my own methadone, but I never thought I'd have to use it. I've used it continuously since I got here. This place is barbaric."

"This is a total nightmare. I just want to go home. I never dreamed it would hurt like this."

"Does it feel like someone has a blowtorch on high on your rear end?" she asked, rubbing her right rear cheek.

"I can't even touch it. It's like fire."

As we commiserated, she continued, "You know, together we make almost a whole person. You have a good right side, and I have a good left." She struggled to get up.

I smiled. "Be careful heading back out that slider. Pigeons are dive bombing to get in here."

"They're in my room too . . . makes it feel really clean, doesn't it?"

We tried to laugh as she hobbled around the corner back to her room, holding on to the walls to keep herself upright.

I heard a knock on my door. It was Thomas, one of the nurses I had met earlier in the day. "Hello, Joanne," he said with a smile, as he peered through the now open door.

"Hey, Thomas, how's it going?"

"It's going?" He was confused.

"Oh, that's just slang for how are you?"

"I am sorry my English is not so good."

"Your English is great, Thomas. You probably just don't get much time to practice."

"I would like very much to practice here with you?"

"Sure, that's fine. But I get tired quickly."

"I must give you a wash, so I'll practice while I'm working." He broke into a huge smile, and his eyes shone.

He was like a little kid, and I hated to disappoint him. "Okay, you can practice while you wash."

"You have something else to change into?" He looked around the room and opened a cupboard.

"You mean pajamas?" He nodded.

"They're in that cupboard over there." I pointed behind him.

As he gathered my pajamas, along with the soap and wash-cloths that my sisters had brought from the hotel, I wondered how this bath thing was going to work. Thomas was male—my previous bath was done by a female nurse, so I assumed there had to be a more modest approach with mixed company. Wrong again. Thomas rolled up a cart with stainless bowls of hot water, took off my pajamas, and proceeded to wash me—exactly the same proce-dure as the female nurse had performed just days before.

Oblivious, Thomas continued to practice his English on me. The whole thing was both nerve-wracking and comical.

My embarrassment lasted for about five minutes, but evapo-rated when I realized how ludicrous it was to worry about modesty. The entire staff had seen more of my naked body in a week than my sweet husband had all last year. I was grateful again that Mike and I had elected for him to stay home with our son rather than travel with me to France. After the naked English lessons, I slept for a long time.

I was awakened by the strong smell of ammonia. The clean-ing lady was mopping the halls outside my room. I reached over to the nightstand and turned on the portable CD player next to my bed. Sounds of the Italian opera star, Andrea Bocelli, filled my room.

The cleaning lady, a big, grinning woman in her midforties with one gold tooth, danced into my room and swooned with her mop. She put her hand to her heart and sighed. We both smiled. Neither of us had spoken a word, but we both under-stood in that beautiful moment how perfectly music transcends all language barriers. When the song finished, she floated off down the hall, and I closed my eyes in thankfulness.

Much to our surprise, I was released from the hospital late in the afternoon of April 28, a mere three days after the third surgery. We were incredulous. As we left the hospital, Patty and Sheila helped me into the back seat of our rental car. I could not sit or put any weight on my rear end or sides, so the only solution was for me to lie on my stomach scrunched in the tiny back seat. With my lower legs bent against the window of the little car, I prayed that Patty would not encounter any bumps in the road as she drove.

With no more room in the car, Bev opted to walk the mile back. I imagined what it might be like to be able to walk for pleasure again.

Will I ever be able to do that again, God?

We later discovered, through a conversation with several members of Dr. Bedeau's team, why Dr. Bedeau had been so nonchalant about my postsurgical hemorrhaging—he didn't know about it. Dr. Bedeau was scrubbing after surgery when Dr. Shafir had discovered the blood-soaked mattress. Dr. Shafir had covered up the extent of my bleeding.

When he learned of my release from the hospital, Philippe, the head surgical nurse, reported the doctor's negligence and cover-up to Dr. Bedeau. Philippe had come to my room to explain to us what had happened when Dr. Shafir walked in on him. Dr. Shafir had warned Philippe to keep his mouth shut. Only when Phillipe was certain no harm would come to Jenna or to me, did he reveal the truth to Dr. Bedeau. Dr. Shafir was fired before we returned to America.

The day Dr. Bedeau found out about my bleeding incident, a nurse was sent from the hospital to our hotel room to take a blood draw. When the results were delivered to me at the hotel, Bev read the grim report: although I was now six days past the hemorrhage, my blood volume was down by more than one-third. Dr. Bedeau never acknowledged the negligence.

"You should have had a transfusion! This is horrible. I don't know how you're going to travel."

"I don't care if I can't walk, sit, or stand. I am going home. I am never going back to that place again."

Finally out of the hospital and away from the threat of further trauma, I rested. Sheila and Patty went out for short day trips when I insisted they take a break from the loathsome memory of the hospital and from me—but Bev would not be swayed. She insisted on staying with me, and I was so thankful that she did.

One day, when Patty and Sheila had gone out to get some fresh air and to pick up some lunch for us, I heard a knock on the door. Jenna, Dr. Bedeau's other American patient, hobbled barefoot into the room past Bev. She had traveled two floors on the elevator and down a very long corridor to see me. She was shaking and her face was gray and pinched from the extraordinary effort. I knew that look.

"I just thought I'd come and check on you. Mind if I lie down in this other bed?" Jenna said.

"No, make yourself comfortable."

"As if that's possible," we said in unison.

"Hey, you two will be all right for a while, right? I'm going to walk down and catch up with Patty and Sheila," Bev said.

"Yeah, of course. I know how exciting it is to listen to us compare horror stories."

"French bistro or relive the nightmare at the hospital? Tough choice!" Bev said as she walked out the door.

I shifted my body a bit to look at Jenna. "I don't know how you made it down here to see me. How's your pain now?"

"It sucks. Methadone is the only way I'm making it. I took some about an hour ago, and that's why I'm here."

"Methadone makes you social?" I said, trying to find something to laugh about.

"It's pretty much the only thing that makes me able to participate in life at all." Jenna groaned as she rubbed the upper part of her right buttock and tried to smile. "This intense stabbing pain in the rear is something, huh?"

"Definitely feels like my left cheek is on a skewer. How long do you think it'll be like this?"

I paused, not wanting to admit what I really thought. "I wish I knew. Right now, I think it was all a big mistake coming here. Maybe, in time, it will have been worth it."

"It's not like we had much choice in the matter. We were flat out of options back in the States." Her angry response startled me, but then she quieted her voice enough to say, "But what happened to you is just horrible. I can't believe what you've been through."

"Yeah," was all I could manage out without crying.

After a few more minutes of exchanging war stories, exhaustion overcame me, and my eyes began to shut. Jenna announced she had to limp back to her room before the Methadone began to wear off.

Later that afternoon, Dr. Bedeau called Sheila on her cell to see if we were up for going out to dinner with him and his wife. She declined gracefully before hanging up. She turned to tell me the nature of his call.

"What?" I was dumbfounded. "Sure, I'll just hop up, put on makeup and my nicest outfit and meet them at a restaurant!"

"I don't think he realizes what bad shape you're in, Joanne," Sheila said.

How could he not realize the shape I'm in? I thought.

I was baffled—it was like living in parallel universes. I had just undergone three surgeries in three days. Dr. Bedeau had sent a nurse to my hotel room to draw my blood for a lab report, the results of which showed major loss of blood consistent with my bleed-out. He had written multiple prescriptions for painkillers, in recognition of my pain-racked state. Now he invites me out to *dinner* for a social evening with his wife?

There is no logic here, God. Nothing makes sense. I just want to go home.

18

Home Sweet Home

Laughter rises out of tragedy when you need it the
most and rewards you for your courage.

—ERMA BOMBECK

The next morning, we began to plan our trip home. *Home.*
What a delicious word.

Bev would depart the following morning from Marseilles,
while Patty, Sheila, and I decided to take the bullet train, avoid-
ing the cramped plane ride from Marseilles to Paris.

Patty and Sheila left to pack the small rental car trunk and
eventually returned to gather me. With the two of them holding
me up, I made my way to the open car door. The pillow Patty
had brought waited for me on the back seat of the car. Shaking,
I lowered myself to the back seat and positioned myself onto
my stomach again. Patty gently folded my legs into the confined
floor space and shut the door.

As soon as the car door was shut I began to cry from both pain and relief. I was so glad to be leaving. I squeezed my eyes against the tears that forced their way down my face. Sheila reached between the seats and passed me tissues.

Dear God, please give me the strength I need to get home. Be with me minute by minute. We returned the car to the rental agency and boarded the bullet train to Paris. Despite being able to lie down the entire way, the trip exhausted me. I was overwrought with pain and trembling uncontrollably from overall weakness.

I saw black spots in front of my eyes and couldn't form a complete thought in my mind. I felt vulnerable, fragile, and unable to predict or manage my own body. *How can I go on, God?*

As we left the rental car agency, Sheila and Patty managed all our luggage and took turns holding me up until we reached the airport terminal. Once inside the Charles de Gaulle Airport, Patty stood in line to check us in while Sheila badgered an airline employee to get a wheelchair for me.

At the flight check-in counter, Patty pointed to me as the ticket agent held up my passport. Holding on to a pole a few feet from the counter, I stood, legs quaking, for the identification procedure. Then I saw the agent nod and smile—either God's mercy prevailed to help me avoid another fray over my passport, or the agent thought I was near death and decided not to hassle us.

Meanwhile, Sheila was told the airline would provide a wheelchair for me, but airport rules required that I be deposited at my gate where I would be transferred to a metal, straight-backed chair. Sitting was the worst position for my pain, but standing was not an option either. With check-in accomplished, Patty joined Sheila in full-scale verbal combat with an airline employee about the wheelchair.

As they grappled with the customer service representative, my pain escalated, and I broke out in a cold sweat. As I exhaled, I felt the last of my strength leave me, and a screen of black veiled my vision. *Oh no, God. I'm passing out.*

I was still trying to cling to the pole when my knees buckled and I began to sink to the floor. Patty ran over to catch me. I felt a wheelchair being pushed under me. My head was still swimming as I was eased into the chair. Patty focused solely on me while the wheelchair operator continued to argue with Sheila. He began to push me toward our gate, but Sheila motioned and told him to follow her. Reluctantly, he obliged.

Sheila navigated us to a manager of the airport. She explained my situation to him, while I slumped in the chair, too exhausted to even look up. The manager said something in French to our wheelchair attendant, and within five minutes we were escorted into the airline's first-class lounge. There, I was offered an overstuffed chair and ottoman to lie down on until our flight departed.

Sitting in the wheelchair had taken its toll on me; my pain level was skyrocketing, and lying on my side was challenging. Patty reached into my purse to find my painkillers. Our wheelchair man was replaced with a concierge for Air France who checked on us often to make sure we had enough drinks and snacks.

"How do you say double gin and tonic in French, Sheila?" Patty laughed.

"You are amazing," she said, and ordered two from the concierge. "We've dealt with enough. We aren't backing down anymore."

It was finally time for us to make our way to the gate. Sheila had made our wheelchair man promise to come back to take us to the gate. He was true to his word, and we arrived at the gate with time to spare. Unfortunately, the wheelchair was too wide to fit on board the plane.

"Are you kidding me?" Sheila cried.

"Typical! Joanne, you are so blessed. I can hardly wait to travel with you again." Patty's sarcasm matched the exasperation in her voice.

A long conversation ensued between Sheila and our wheel-chair man's boss via his two-way radio. Sheila's French flowed with fiery determination. Patty and I didn't need to speak the language to understand what she was saying.

"Wow," Patty said, with raised eyebrows.

In less than five minutes, several airline personnel came and escorted us through a series of doors and hallways. We eventually found ourselves outside the gate on the tarmac.

"What are we doing here?" I said, setting my jaw against my mounting pain.

"Apparently, there is no easy way to get you on the plane because of the size of your wheelchair," Sheila said, yelling over the noise of the plane's engines. "It's too far for you to walk, so they are going to board you on the plane with some sort of hydraulic vehicle that brings supplies to the cargo door."

"This ought to be good," Patty said, choking back laughter.

Around the corner came a large rectangular-shaped vehicle that looked as if it had been run over by a few airplanes. Part truck and part lift, the platform on the back looked to be the same dimensions as a king-size mattress. The maintenance man, clad in blue coveralls, took my hand while he pushed my chair to the side of the platform. He strapped me into a gray harness and told me not to move. As if I had any strength to do so.

Patty and Sheila held on to a horizontal metal bar that

stretched the length of the vehicle. Their shoulders shook with laughter. I managed a weak smile at the absurdity of it all, although I felt the small amount of strength I had gained in the airport lounge slipping away. How would I ever withstand this journey?

The loud groaning and grinding of gears jolted me from my uncertainty. With a huge jerk we were finally moving forward. Minutes later, the hydraulic mechanism lifted us up until we were even with the door of the enormous aircraft. I watched Patty and Sheila convulse into new fits of laughter.

The watchful maintenance man held his grit-encrusted palm in front of my face for a moment, letting me know I was not to move. I was slumped against the harness and not going anywhere. He ushered Patty and Sheila off the platform, then returned with a strange looking wheelchair—skinny with a tall metal back.

"Why couldn't this smaller wheelchair have been brought to the terminal in the first place, so I could have skipped the ride on the delivery platform?" I said to no one in particular.

With gentle care, the maintenance man transferred me into the new chair and proceeded onto the plane. At first he tried to push me down the aisle facing forward, but the chair banged into people's legs, arms, and seatbacks. All eyes were on us. While he labored and sweated, my pain spiked out of control. I bit my tongue and cried fresh rivers of tears. My determined helper backed all the way out onto the platform and began again, with me facing backward this time.

Because of the trail of bruised elbows and ankles we had created on our first attempt, most of the passengers in the outside seats now stood and watched as I was pulled down the aisle. If I had not been in so much pain, I would have remarked to the onlookers about the ferocious way my maintenance man protected me.

When at last he deposited me into seats 23B and C, spontaneous applause broke out for my maintenance man. Sheila and Patty tried to give him money, but he wouldn't take it. Teary and shaking, I barely had enough strength to mutter an intelligible thank you.

I lay down on my side on my two seats with my feet in Patty's lap. The French flight attendants came by several times before takeoff to make sure I was comfortable. From the looks on their faces, I must have looked ghastly. Throughout the flight, they were very attentive—quite a contrast to our previous flights.

Nevertheless, it was a grueling eight-hour trip. When we touched down in Boston, I shed more tears.

I'm thankful, God. I'm thankful. It was all I could express.

⇒⥼⇐

Patty's husband, Mark, greeted us. He had fitted their SUV with a twin mattress topper, pillows, and blankets. He helped me slide gently onto the makeshift bed in the back and then loaded our bags. Sheila and Patty looked weary.

"We're almost there, girls," Shelia said as she slid into the back seat.

Limping into Mark and Patty's living room with the two of them holding me up, I noticed a twin bed in the middle of the room.

"Redecorating, Mark?" I tried a weak smile at my lame joke.

"Yeah, yeah, just for you, Joanne. It's your place of rest for the next few days. Since you can't do stairs and the bathroom and kitchen are both close, I thought this would work best."

"You guys are incredible," I said as I collapsed onto the bed. I was asleep in seconds.

Sheila was gone when I awoke but had left word with Patty that she would come by before my return home.

Mom arrived a few days later to help me return to California. I was overjoyed to see her and dissolved into an emotional mess as she folded me into her arms. She brought new energy and strength into my recovery process. I could breathe easier knowing that Patty's stress would be lifted with someone there to share the burden.

The sounds of laughter during dinner preparations drew me into the kitchen. After the ordeal in France, I longed to participate in something ordinary and feel normal again. I limped into the kitchen, expecting to share in the raucous party atmosphere my family typically creates during mealtime. Everyone, including my seventeen-year-old nephew, immediately ordered me back to bed. I was too weak to be up, and I knew they were right.

Back in my bed, I smiled as I listened to the hilarity in the kitchen. I drifted off to sleep again, musing over the enormous sacrifices my family had made for me over the years. For this reason alone I am blessed.

Sheila came by that evening to say goodbye. As Patty and Mom hauled groceries in from the car, I had a chance to speak to her privately.

"Sheila, I don't know how to thank you. Without you, I am certain I would not be here now. God used you to save my life." She took my hands in hers, and our eyes filled with tears at the memory of all we had been through.

"I think about the timing of the food poisoning a lot. I know, without a doubt, that it was God who told me to get to the hospital. He really wanted you to make it. Being around you, Jo, has increased my faith and given me a desire to know God better. I am grateful to you for letting me be part of your journey."

We hugged goodbye.

Sheila is the embodiment of selflessness and a carrier of God's presence. The world needs more Sheilas in it.

≫⟨

A few days later at sunrise, Mom and I prepared for the journey back to Sacramento. My bags were packed with large amounts of opiate pain pills from both America and France. I was relieved that my passport did not have to be inspected again. I planned to light it on fire when I returned home.

For this flight, Mom and I had first-class tickets. I hoped and prayed I would make the journey without collapsing from pain. With no one behind me, and Mom to my right, I reclined fully and lay on my right side. Mom worried over me constantly.

"Let me put another pillow under your hip," she said.

"No, I'm okay with this pad and the blanket behind me, thanks, Mom."

"You don't look okay; let me get another blanket for you," she insisted. "I'll put it behind your back, and it will help keep you on your side."

I sighed. "Okay." I would let Mom mother so I could be done with expending energy in conversation. I said a silent prayer: *Thank you, God, for giving me such a kind mom. Please relieve her fear and anxiety over me as she trusts in You.*

We were both glad for the distraction of a young man traveling with his tiny dog in a carrier under his seat. I rested as Mom listened to his life story and how he and his dog, Roscoe, had come to be best buddies.

When he was finished, Mom launched into the fifteen-minute version of why we were traveling and my ordeal in France. Roscoe's owner looked horrified. Mom seemed oblivious that she had thoroughly grossed out the poor man and had caused me to have to relive the ordeal. The young man and I let out audible sighs of relief when the captain announced our descent. *Thank You, God, that we are landing.* I wanted to be as far away from my experience in France as possible.

We were the last ones to leave the plane. As we slowly made our way to the baggage claim, I reached into my purse to grab more pain meds and a piece of gum. When I tried to shove the gum into my mouth, I realized I had clamped my jaw into lockdown mode during the flight because of my escalating pain. Now I could not open my mouth wide enough to get the gum in. I settled for a narrow breath mint and hoped a pair of pliers might work to open my jaw when I got home.

As we descended from the baggage claim area on the escalator, I heard my son, Kian.

"Mom, over here!" He yelled and waved frantically while jumping up and down. Mike stood next to him with a broad smile. Standing there were the two reasons I had made my choice in my conversation with God.

When we reached the bottom, six-year-old Kian ran into my arms. Mike wrapped his arms around me, and I knew in my spirit that only God could have gotten me through such a horrendous journey. Despite the tremendous pain I was in as I stood there, I had an overwhelming sense of peace that my choice had been the right one for this time and place. Our family was back together, and I was going to make it—*we* were going to make it.

"Mom, Mom, I missed you so much. You were gone such a long time! How was your trip? Did they fix your pelvis pain? I've been so excited to see you. Grandma and Grandpa are at our house, and they're making it nice for you. Why are you crying, Mom?" His words tumbled faster and faster from his mouth.

I dropped to my knees. "I missed you, too, sweetie! I am so happy to be home," I said as I pulled him tighter to me. Kian reached up and placed his palms on my cheeks and pulled my face to his.

"Oh, Mom, I hope they fixed your pelvis pain and you don't have to go away like that again. Dad and me miss you too much," he said as he squeezed me with all his might.

"I love you so much, buddy," I said as I nearly squeezed the breath from him.

Silently I prayed. *God, thank You for the prayers of the saints. Thank You for their faithful intercession for me. Thank You for Your abounding love and mercy in giving me a choice to come back and raise this little boy along with my husband. I cannot imagine what it would have been like for them if the news had been that I was never coming home.*

Finally able to release my grip on Kian, I allowed Mike to help me to my feet and hold me next to him. Leaning into my husband's strength infused me with new courage.

With our luggage collected, Mike hurried us out the door to the van. He had prepared the back of our car in the same way Mark had when we landed in Boston. Kian begged for permission to lie down beside me on the van bed. After being away for a month and living through hell, I could not be bothered with seatbelt laws. I said yes, and we both settled in, lying on our sides as the van pulled away from the curb.

Mom and Mike chatted in the front while Kian continued to ask me every question he could think of, all the while gripping my hand between the two of his. Mike's parents, Darrell

19

It Takes a Village

Never believe that a few caring people can't change the
world. For, indeed, that is all who ever have.

—MARGARET MEAD, CULTURAL ANTHROPOLOGIST

I made you some custard, Jo, and left it in the fridge. Your mom says you aren't eating much, and I know that's something you like." Roberta leaned down to hug me goodbye. "We're so glad you're home. I'll be praying. You've been through so much. Darrel and I will come back when your mom has to return to Florida."

Darrel waved to me from the bedroom doorway. "You take care of yourself. I washed the windows so you can see that orchid blooming outside. I hung it on the tree out there."

"You guys are wonderful. Thanks for taking such good care of Kian and Mike and everything else around here," I said.

When Darrel and Roberta left, my mom took over caring for us. The following day she drove me to my primary care doctor to make sure I didn't need a blood transfusion. The bloodwork showed I had hemoglobin levels below 8.0; normal range is from 12.0 to 15.5. My doctor, Mom, and I discussed possible next steps.

The doctor said I should have had a transfusion in France, and at this point my need was borderline. With rest and proper nutrition, he believed my body would eventually repair the lost volume on its own. We agreed to wait and that I would return in ten days to repeat the bloodwork.

⸙

Getting acclimated to life after France was exhausting. I remained weak, fatigued, and in so much pain I slept much of the time. I wondered if I would ever regain my strength and be free from pain. It consumed my every moment. To manage the effects of the trauma I had endured, I wanted to shove everything about that agony away from me and pretend everything was good.

My friends and family were selfless—out of love they supported me, encouraged me, and prayed for me. Still, I had a deep need to interact with the people I loved the way I did before I was injured. Every relationship had taken a back seat to the demands of my condition and pain management. I craved to be normal; I missed the ordinary rhythms of engaging with people I cared about.

In the past, many people had offered to help as I recovered from my surgeries. I had mostly refused their help because I knew I could not reciprocate or even manage the demands of a conversation that came with the offers of assistance. After France, however, God had been teaching me the value of receiving. I resolved to try to be a friend who could receive the expressions of friendship. My near-death experience and encounter with God gave me a new appreciation, as well as a rare understanding of how precious and fleeting life was.

During my second week at home, I shared my near-death experience with a few close friends. As I did so, it became clear that my encounter with God had not been for my benefit alone. This realization emboldened me to tell my story to others.

One day, my former Bible study leader brought a load of gourmet-quality food to our house for our dinner. I was lying in my bed when she came to the bedroom doorway.

"I promise not to stay too long. I've been praying and praying for you. How are you doing right now?" she asked, leaning into the doorframe.

"It's painful, but I'm so grateful to be home." I motioned for her to sit on my bed.

While our conversation continued, I felt a prompting to share the amazing experience God had given me. I tried to choke back the flood of tears as I began to tell her what had happened. I had to stop often through the retelling of my near-death experience to compose myself.

Her mouth fell open, and she began to cry.

"Oh, my gosh! What a gift! I mean, I know we are called to pray for each other, but I never dreamed our prayers mattered like this. I'm overwhelmed."

I could only nod in response.

"I'm so sorry for all you have suffered, Joanne, but I am grateful that God allowed you to come back to share this amazing testimony with the rest of us," she said without pausing to breathe. "I have had such a difficult time lately with health and family challenges, but after hearing this, I feel like I never want to stop praying."

"I am so thankful for your prayers. God truly listens. I know the prayers of all of you changed everything for me."

"Is it okay if I share this with our Bible study leadership team?" she asked. "I wish you could share it, but I know you'll be out awhile and I think this is something they need to hear now."

I nodded as she stood up to leave. We hugged goodbye.

God, thank You for using my pain and my story to bring encouragement to all those who hear it. Let their faith and hope in Your supernatural power and love be increased.

⋙⋘

At the end of two weeks, Mom needed to go home, so Roberta came back again. Bev flew in and tagged Roberta after another week. When Bev had to return to work the following week, my friend Scotti came up from Los Angeles. My family and I received a constant stream of support like this for months.

After about three months, I was finally able to drive very short distances that lasted five to eight minutes, all the while sitting on my blue cushion. Even with the strongest pain meds, sitting more than that amount of time would cause a tremendous pain flare-up that could last for more than a week.

Although my body was still ravaged by pain and fatigue, and my emotional state was tender, I experienced a spiritual consistency that I had not known before. I needed God more and more. I knew there was more to know about Him. I yearned to look at Jesus and experience the fullness of His love as I had when He spoke to me in France.

God had given me a clear message during my near-death experience. He had allowed me to choose life here on earth. Now I needed Him to help me figure out how to live it supernaturally because my natural life was seeped with physical torment. I feared if I took my eyes off Him and focused on my circumstances I would be overcome with bitterness.

When my strength returned, I began getting up at 4:30 every morning to spend hours with God. Even in my pain, I made myself go to God in worship and to meditate on His Word. As I worshipped and yielded to Him, I experienced more of His presence. I practiced hearing, seeing, yielding, and surrendering.

Through my obedience, I began to fall more deeply in love with God and to know His love for me in profound ways. At times it was a huge struggle for me to engage with Him. At other times He would come to me and would share amazing things, leaving me with no words to explain my affection and delight. Slowly I began to see who God is and who He said I am, and this kept His Word alive in me. My passion for Him was born from obedience to Him. In the natural it didn't make sense but supernaturally, it changed everything.

One morning I read Psalm 5:1–3 in *The Message* version of the Bible.

> Listen, GOD! Please, pay attention!
> Can you make sense of these ramblings,
> my groans and cries?
> King-God, I need your help.
> Every morning
> you'll hear me at it again.
> Every morning
> I lay out the pieces of my life
> on your altar
> and watch for fire to descend.

I understood the desperation of King David's heart to hear from God and to see Him act. When we reach our own end, God is right there to give us a beginning in Him. I prayed I would never lose my desperation for God.

Coming to Him daily in that early morning quiet place helped me to focus on the person of God. When I looked at His majesty, nature, and character, I knew His promise to be with me "minute by minute" was true. I learned I could grasp God's voice with my heart. His presence, His voice, and His love were so indescribable I would leave the encounters overwhelmed with peace. His peace was vital if I was to navigate my days. I had to decide every day to yield to God.

⁂

Twelve weeks post-op, I received a survey in the mail from Dr. Bedeau. It grieved me to check the box marked "no improvement." Moreover, I had to admit that I was much worse than I had been before the surgeries. In a subsequent e-mail exchange with Dr. Bedeau, he assured me not to give up hope, saying my case was one of the worst he had ever treated. He hoped in several months I would notice the nerve pain begin to die as normal nerve pathways were being regenerated. I prayed for that day and tried to believe what he told me.

By early fall, my pain was under control for a short period of time early in the day, due to an increase in the amounts of narcotic pain medication I could take. I experienced pain control until about ten o'clock in the morning, after which a fiery pain would spiral like a fury unleashed until the next morning. It was like chasing after a tornado—I had no ability to catch it.

Some days, I resumed a few light household duties during

those few morning hours until the pain became unbearable. Mike, now working more than seventy hours a week at his demanding job, would step in to get dinner or to help with Kian. I felt tremendous guilt over my inability to contribute to our household, and it broke my heart to watch my husband carry the load that should have been mine. There were days when I couldn't get a handle on pain control at all. Then, faced with debilitating pain, I would crawl back into bed or sit in a scalding bath multiple times during the day.

The desire to be "normal" reared within me—twisting me up inside until my next meeting with God the following morning. With pain continuing at unbearable levels, I had no real quality of life. My entire existence was reduced to simply making it through the day—one minute at a time. I trusted God and loved Him deeply because of the richness of my relationship with Him, but still I grappled with how to cope. I was keeping my eyes on Jesus, but I was living with a vicious cycle of pain, and it was exhausting.

By this time I was taking three different opiate medications for pain control, as well as medication for sleep because pain kept me awake during the night. I was also using a TENS Unit (electrical stimulation for muscles) and seeing a chiropractor. A massage therapist came to the house once a week to help relieve the tension in my back.

I had compensated for years of pain in the way I walked, sat, and stood. This, in turn, caused tremendous pressure on the right side of my body. When I stood, I placed most of my weight on my right foot. When I sat, I placed all my weight on my right buttock only. These therapeutic measures helped me to cope momentarily but had no lasting effect.

I began to have trouble with acid reflux and fluid buildup

in my lungs because I was unable to eat sitting straight up. I developed bronchitis. I choked through the night and used bed pillows to prop me up, but that only exacerbated the pain in my back and pelvis. I was reluctant to increase the amount of narcotic pain medication I was taking any more than necessary as the side effect of constipation exacerbated my nerve pain. Medication for my lungs and stomach added to my arsenal of prescription drugs. I felt my body breaking down piece by piece.

Mike heated flannel bags filled with flax seed and gave them to me before bed every night. The heat offered some relief, enabling me to fall asleep for a few hours.

With no lasting improvement in sight, I decided to increase the dosage of narcotic medication I was taking. In addition, my doctor prescribed a fourth narcotic medication for increased coverage. To counteract the side effect of constipation, he increased the strength of the prescription laxatives I was taking. As a result, I suffered through anal spasms that sent me crashing to the floor in agony. My pain management doctor suggested new drugs from time to time, and I tried them all.

Early one morning I couldn't resist an overwhelming urge to do something normal for my son, so I took Kian to an early movie five minutes away. I knew I couldn't sit through the film, but the desperation to do something with my son that other parents did for their children overrode my common sense.

"Mom, this is the greatest thing ever! We are going to see a movie! I can't wait. Aren't you excited?" Kian chattered nonstop. He loved going anywhere.

"Yes, sweetie. I think we'll have a blast." I tried to convince myself as I said the words.

I sat down in the theater and immediately knew I had made a mistake. I retreated to the back of the room and squatted down against the wall. Kian stood next to me with his arm on my shoulder, eyes focused on the screen. I tried not to cry. He never questioned why we moved around during the movie and happily adapted to whatever posture suited me.

I thanked God for my little boy who brought me so much joy. He was a daily reminder of God's grace and reinforced my commitment to continue to fight the pain that consumed me. In these moments, I held on to God's promise that He would never leave me. He was my lifeboat escape from my sinking Titanic of an existence.

20

Shop 'Til You Drop

You've got bad eating habits if you use a grocery cart in 7-Eleven.
—DENNIS MILLER, COMEDIAN

When I dropped off Kian at school in the early mornings, I prayed, more often than not, that I wouldn't run into anyone I knew. I took pain pills twenty minutes before leaving the house so I could drive the short distance. Students had to be walked to their classrooms, and I wore sunglasses as I walked through the school buildings and back to my car. Tears burned the back of my eyelids when the pain was intolerable. I feared someone might ask, just at that moment, how I was doing.

One morning, about to escape the school grounds, I had my hand on the handle of my car door when the mother of a friend of Kian's stopped me.

"Hi, Joanne, you look like you're not walking very well. How are you doing?"

"Hi, Margie, I'm—"

I couldn't finish my sentence. Her question unleashed an avalanche of raw emotion, and my eyes filled. I was shocked that her simple question about my health would cause such an emotional upheaval. I didn't know how to respond for fear of going to pieces.

"I'm so sorry. Please let us know if there is anything we can do for you," she said as she reached out to hug me.

"Thanks, Margie. I can't stand here; my pain level is too high. Let's talk later." My voice cracked as I opened my car door with shaking hands. I noticed the front of my T-shirt was covered in large wet blotches as tears ran down my face.

Margie nodded and waved as I drove away sobbing. I prayed as I drove. *What if this will be the way it always is, Father? How will I go on?* The memory of my encounter with God in France flooded back to me. Again I heard His voice promising me, "I will be with you minute by minute...."

Peace slowly crept in, and I realized I must continue to take each day one minute at a time. I would find God's strength as I reached for Him for one minute and then another. I didn't see a shortcut. My disability was training me to have total dependence on God. The Bible was clear about being reliant on God.

I recalled the words of Jesus:

> Our Father which art in heaven, Hallowed be thy
> name.
> Thy kingdom come, Thy will be done in earth, as it is
> in heaven.
> Give us this day our daily bread.... (Matthew 6:9–11
> KJV)

He didn't ask for us to pray to be given a week or a month or a lifetime of provision but simply for this day; a day that unfolds one minute at a time—minute by minute.

As I pulled onto the freeway, I thought about what living moment to moment really meant. All my adult life I had been a planner, setting and obtaining huge goals, always living in the future. Existing this way allowed me to feel in control of my life at all times. I believed in the sovereignty of God, but I also believed that setting goals was the sure way to create my own destiny.

The words God spoke to me during my ordeal in France were teaching me to remain focused on being content in the moment. Pain had become my greatest teacher, forcing me to remain fully in the present all the time. I could know content- ment amid excruciating pain when I concentrated on God and the promises in His Word. The moment I thought about what the future held for me, I would be overcome with fear and anxi- ety. In the present, faith and hope were obtainable.

⇟⇞

Grocery shopping became the bane of my existence. Although Mike or other family members and friends usually helped, now and then I tried to shop in the early morning to gauge any improvement in my stamina and pain. It was a balancing act from the start—the size of the store, the act of shopping, loading and unloading the car, and putting away groceries all figured into the equation.

The large warehouse stores offered cheaper pricing, but I soon learned they were too immense for me to tackle. I often made it to the checkout line with a full cart only to end up abandoning it to head to my car as pain engulfed me. Since I couldn't sit, the motorized shopping carts were of no use to me. The times I made it through my full grocery list in a midsized store, I was unable to load the car and unpack the groceries when I returned home.

To help our financial situation, which continued to be challenged by all my medical expenses, I vowed to overcome my pain and shop at a new warehouse grocery store that opened at 8:00 a.m. I reasoned I could manage the shopping experience as long as I was home and lying down by 10:00 a.m.

Kian had pointed the store out to me from the freeway as we drove by every day on the way home from school. He loved reading the posted signs and often asked me what this store was. My friends all shopped there and remarked it wasn't as big as Costco. I decided to shop there and prove to myself that I wasn't in as bad shape as I thought. Convinced that this store would help solve the Moody household monthly financial strain, I soldiered into the new giant food store with Kian by my side and my pain meds at their peak.

The size of the carts alarmed me—as big as the colossal ones at Costco. The first cart I chose had a faulty wheel that pulled me to the left, causing it to smack into the sliding door entrance. Sweat broke out on my upper lip. I took a deep breath and determined I would not be defeated at the store entrance. I switched to another cart. Kian immediately squatted down next to the wheels.

"This one looks okay, Mom."

"Okay, honey, let's go," I said, trying to match his exuberance. I moved past the glass doors where the sight of hundreds of giant boxes towering above greeted me with instant intimidation. The box fronts had been cut away displaying thousands of cans organized in rows and piled halfway to the forty-foot ceilings.

"Not a good sign," I said to Kian with a sigh.

"Wow! Oh, Mom, isn't it great we're finally shopping here? Look at all these cans stacked up!" he replied, oblivious to my rising anxiety.

Kian loved going anywhere, and, being especially fond of food, he could not think of a better outing for us. I smiled at his elation and pushed the cart to the produce section.

I need to buy only twelve onions to really save some money here, I thought. How many onions can a family of three eat in a week?

Kian was at the end of the aisle looking at a squashed grape on the floor and was oblivious to my increasing pain.

Since I wasn't planning to make onion soup, I settled for two onions for the price of ten. I rounded the corner and saw the lay of the land—this store was the size of Texas! The sweat from my upper lip began a slow descent down the creases next to my mouth. I steeled myself against the desire to run out of the store.

"Mom, look at all the rows we can go up and down! This is going to be great," Kian said as he took my hand and began pulling me and the mammoth cart down the first aisle.

I lost Kian at the bulk items section as he ooohed and ahhhed his way around barrel after barrel of candy—licorice, gumdrops, taffy, and more. You name it, they carried it in volume. This rainbow assortment of pure sugar mixed with food dye could put the healthiest kid into a diabetic coma. I knew if I didn't make it to the dairy and meat section soon I would be done for at the checkout line.

I called Kian away from the candy and moved more quickly to fill the cart with the remaining items on our shopping list. I tried to find any remnant of a stomach muscle to help me lift the items into the cart. Legs in a straddle, I used what little leg strength I had to keep the cart from wobbling side to side. I finally had Kian stand next to me and help push the cart forward. After a near collision with a display of relish, I declined Kian's offer of further help and loaded the cart with chicken, milk, and yogurt. Finally, I reached the checkout line.

"You can do it, come on," I kept repeating silently to myself. I swallowed three more pain pills without water and prayed they would help. Suddenly fire erupted in my pelvis. The insidious creep of nerve pain began to fill my lower abdomen and vaginal canal. I refused to let this shopping trip be in vain, so I threw the items onto the conveyor belt. I didn't understand how to check out at this store, and the checker offered no help. My friend had told me you had to bag your own groceries, but that didn't sound like a big deal. I saw other shoppers at the end of their conveyor belts, loading their groceries into plastic bags. I moved down to the end of the black belt and attempted to do the same.

"Hit the hip pad," the clerk yelled over her shoulder.

"What?" I yelled back.

"The hip pad," she said again, without even glancing in my direction. I was baffled. Shrugging off the perplexing instructions, I noticed that my groceries weren't moving down the belt but remained piled up near the checker. She glared at me, and then the items finally began to move. Faster and faster they came. While I threw the items into bags, Kian wandered over to the candy display across from the checker.

"Mom, can I have this gum and this 3 Musketeers bar?" He held one each in his little fists.

"No, you don't need those," I said.

"Mom! It's only two things!" he demanded.

"Put that back and come over here!" I yelled a little too loudly.

"Mom, please, I want this." His voice quavered.

"No, Kian. We have to go."

I turned to look squarely at him while the groceries crashed into each other. Kian began to cry. My pelvis felt like molten lava, and I was about to cry. The clerk put a divider on the belt and yelled for me to pay. With Kian crying and tears leaking out of the corners of my eyes, I slid my credit card. It was declined.

"We don't take Visa or MasterCard," the checker said with her mouth drawn tight.

Other shoppers in our line stared at me. The woman next to me crossed her arms across her chest. I fumbled for my debit card, slid it into the machine, and felt my insides implode as the screen in front of me read: OVER LIMIT. The line had increased to six people, and the checker turned to face me.

"I'll just write a check," I croaked.

The checker snatched the check from my shaking hand while I snatched the candy and gum from Kian's hands. As I tried to pull my child and the cart away from the checkout stand, I noticed a black pad with two large words: "HIP PAD."

"You've got to be kidding me," I mumbled. "How did I miss that?"

With both of us crying, Kian and I headed to the car. We sobbed the entire way home. Kian sobbed over lost gum, and I sobbed for more reasons than I could count.

When we arrived home, there seemed to be fewer bags to unload for the number of groceries I had purchased. In the store I was convinced I had bought enough to sustain a third-world country. In too much pain to fully analyze the situation, I quickly put only the perishable items away, turned on the television for Kian, and headed for the bathtub.

When Mike returned home that evening, I explained my disastrous attempt at shopping.

"Honey, I'm so sorry. Maybe you need to give up the shopping idea and just let me try and do it all on the weekends."

We had this dialogue often. The guilt I owned from Mike doing everything was too much to bear. Guilt drove me back to the stores. He rummaged through the refrigerator. "Did you get cheese today?"

"Yes, I bought a two-pound block of mild cheddar. Isn't it in there?" I answered as I got up from the couch. "Have some chips, and I'll look for it."

"Where are the chips?" he said as he rummaged through the cabinet.

"I bought a bag of lime-flavored tortilla chips. They must be on the counter still," I said.

Suddenly I recalled, one by one, all the items I purchased that I didn't remember bagging. I burst into tears for the second time that day as I described to Mike the scene at the checkout. He calmly called the store and explained to the manager that we were missing a fair amount of groceries.

"It happens all the time, Mr. Moody. The conveyor belt divides to expedite the bagging process. Your wife must not have noticed that part of her groceries went over to the other side of the belt," he told Mike. "We have the groceries here in the refrigerated section ready for you to pick up."

"I'll be right back," Mike said as he walked out the door to the garage. He was still dressed in his dress shirt and slacks from work.

"Stupid store," I said to Kian. "How would any sane mother even without pelvic pain be able to navigate such an idiotic setup?" I fumed, as I limped back to the couch.

"Expedite the bagging process? I would need nine arms to expedite the process," I mumbled to myself.

Kian looked up from the Lego set he was building. "It was fun shopping there, Mom. Let's go again."

The perspective of this child amazed me. I could change a thing or two about my attitude if I looked at things through his eyes. Instead, I winced and pulled the warm flax bag over my lower abdomen.

We will never go there again, I thought.

Mike returned home with no fewer than six bags of groceries. What a glaring reminder of the tidal wave of agony that had driven me over the edge. Still, it unnerved me that I had left that many groceries behind. Mike and Kian had chips and cheese for dinner. I ate pain pills.

The invention of grocery home delivery finally saved me. Even the mistake of receiving someone else's bag of Fruit Loops, canned salmon, and diapers could not dampen my enthusiasm for this new service. One call to the store, and someone came and picked up the unwanted items. Fantastic!

21

The Power of Surrender

*When you get into a tight space and everything goes
against you . . . never give up then, for that is just
the place and time that the tide will turn.*

—HARRIET BEECHER STOWE

Another difficult summer passed. The months following the
surgery dragged on with no noticeable improvement in my
condition. Our family was fortunate to have Roberta, Bev, Patty,
and Mom visit us at regular intervals to help me get more rest.
They each took Kian to new places and brought laughter into
our home. Every visit was a gift from God, and I was thankful
for the continuous stream of love and support.

My physical limitations frustrated me. I battled ongoing
feelings of self-reproach because Mike was working so hard to
pay for my medications and treatments. I struggled with my
inability to do more with Kian and to participate fully in the

activities of life. I mourned the loss of being able to play piano and sing. I grieved my inability to earn a living and contribute financially to our household.

By early-September 2006, I began developing almost daily anal spasms on my right side. Having exhausted all my options, I decided to try physical therapy again. I found a pelvic pain specialty group for women in downtown Sacramento and determined to go two times a week. My medical insurance wasn't contracted with the group, so, after seeing the first bill, Mike and I knew we couldn't afford it long term. We decided I would go once a week for six weeks. If I had some improvement from the therapy, we would find a way to pay for it.

When I arrived for my visits, I would squat in the waiting room until my name was called. No matter who was working behind the counter, there would always be a remark about how the pudendal nerve patients were easy to identify because we all came in and squatted down against the walls instead of standing or sitting.

When I arrived for my fourth visit, I went first to the bathroom before my treatment (I have learned that a pit stop is necessary when medical professionals are about to commence poking around my bladder area). I was then escorted to the therapy room and left in privacy to change. I climbed up on the table with the gown facing backward and an extra-long sheet draped over my legs. There was even a little foot heater at the end of the exam table.

While lying there I flashed back to my first visit with the surgeon in France. This definitely beat the naked, spread-eagle, exams without sheets I had there. My physical therapist could give a lesson on patient care and comfort to the folks in France. My reflections were soon interrupted by a light knock on the door. There she was.

"Are you ready?" she asked.

While the physical therapist worked on me, she kept using the phrase, "This will be mildly uncomfortable." It's hard to imagine any physical therapy of the vaginal and anal canals that could be called mild. I had the uncomfortable part down pat and wondered when the mildly part might kick in.

I had learned from my left-side nerve treatment that if pelvic floor dysfunction is caught very early and specialized physical therapy is administered, the patient stands a good chance of getting better and not developing painful nerve entrapment. Unfortunately, I didn't receive an early diagnosis, so I was battling extreme odds.

I became concerned that my new symptoms might be an indication that I was developing nerve entrapment on the right side. When painful spasms sent me crashing to the floor, I tried to steer my thoughts away from my fear that I could be facing pudendal nerve surgery all over again. The cycle of constipation and anal spasms suppressed my appetite, so I also began to rapidly lose weight. The pattern was hauntingly familiar. I panicked.

Six weeks of physical therapy came and went with no real improvement in my condition. Just driving home from the clinic sparked the nerve into an inferno. I could not ignore the warning signs any longer. A nerve latency test was ordered in mid-September 2006 in Sacramento. I had endured the latency test more times than I could recall. Steeling myself for that torture again was almost more than I could bear.

On the day of the test, I shook uncontrollably as I got onto the exam table. I relived all the trauma from the other tests as the same agony was inflicted on me once again. The pain was excruciating. I felt as if someone had kicked me in the stomach and forever knocked the wind out of me. I could not take a breath. I balled my hands into fists and fought the urge to scream. Tears ran down and flooded my ears as I lay on my back listening to the doctor's words.

"There is a marked increase in the right side, Joanne. I'm sorry. You are reporting 7.8 with normal being 3. The report I received from Dr. West stated your right side was registering as normal after your surgery in France, so your symptoms of anal spasms and increased pain are confirmed as indicative of entrapment," the doctor said.

My worst fear spoken aloud. I was in too much shock to respond.

"The best chance of beating this is to return to France and have the surgery done again—this time on your right side," he said before he got up and left the room.

I lay on the examining table for a while longer, sobbing bitterly. The nurse stood beside me and gently squeezed my hand. I looked up at her and watched a tear roll down her kind face. She told me how sorry she was, but I was not comforted. My heart grew cold within me, and I fought to keep from going mad with fear.

God, why? Why did You allow me to live? I cried silently.

The nurse left the room, and I moved off the table in slow motion and stepped unsteadily into my clothes. *This must be a nightmare, and I'll wake up soon.*

I did not want to go on. No depth of love for my child, my husband, or family could give me the desire to walk through that fire again. Darkness engulfed me. I swallowed more pain pills and drove home in silence. An ice-cold numbness had settled in my heart.

※

By the spring of 2007, my pain had escalated to such a high level that I was unable to control or endure it. The surgeons I consulted discussed a desperate treatment option—cutting the pudendal nerve. They weren't entirely sure that dissecting the deeply embedded nerve would eliminate the pain, since the pudendal nerve connects to so many other nerve pathways. There wasn't enough research to demonstrate its effectiveness. One thing was certain; the surgery would render me incontinent with a colostomy bag.

My own pain management doctor advised against the surgery. A man of faith, he was convinced that God had allowed me to remain here so others would see God's hand in my life. He also believed I was too young to incur the risks of this surgery.

After months of prayer and meetings with different doctors, I decided to contact Dr. Connor. Dr. Connor was the ob-gyn who had accompanied Jenna to France when we had our surgeries. He was now specializing in pudendal decompression surgery on the East Coast, bringing the techniques of Bedeau's team to the United States. Jenna told me I would be in great hands with Dr. Connor. She invited me to stay with her family while I recovered from the surgery. I didn't need to take her up on her generosity because Patty's home was only an hour's drive away from Dr. Connor's practice.

I didn't want to burden Patty and her family again. She had been through so much with me the last time. I offered to stay in a hotel, but she insisted I stay with her. She and Mark had just built a beautiful lakefront home and were keen to organize outdoor adventures for Kian while I recovered. The thought of having Kian there made me smile. He had so much enthusiasm for life—listening to him tell stories about new adventures would be a great distraction for me as I convalesced.

My phone consultation with Dr. Connor took place on Tuesday afternoon.

"Hi, Dr. Connor, I am not sure you remember me. I was in France when you brought Jenna to have surgery."

"Hi, Joanne, I remember you very well. You really had a time of it over there."

"Yeah, I'm still not over it. I am petrified about any additional surgery. I'm even freaked having this conversation about it. So, before we talk about my right-side entrapment, I am hoping you can help me understand what went wrong in France. Why did I have the bleed?"

"Joanne, if you weren't scared to death I would be shocked. I know you went through hell, but what happened to you is very uncommon. Because of the level of damage to your left side pudendal nerve, Dr. Bedeau decided to use a new internal surgical adhesive instead of traditional sutures. He thought it would give you the best option for minimal scarring along the nerve canal, maintaining a wider opening around the nerve.

"With the four pudendal nerve patients he operated on that week—and remember I was in the operating suite with him—you were the only one he used the adhesive on. Bedeau said you had one of the worst cases of entrapment that he had ever seen, and he was trying to give you the best chance for success. Because the adhesive was a new technique, he had no idea it wouldn't hold around the artery."

"Wow! That explains a lot. Thank you for filling in all the gaps about what happened to me. I am never going outside the US for surgery again," I said.

"I understand. Going to France for surgery is extremely difficult even when there aren't any complications. Listen, if you decide to have the right side done, I will take good care of you. I want to be completely candid here. I don't have the experience level of the surgeons in France, but I have been an ob-gyn surgeon for more than twenty-five years. You will be the eighteenth patient I have performed decompression surgery on. All of them have gone well. You have my word that I will do the very best I can for you."

I felt his genuine warmth, concern, and confidence. Any doctor who would accompany his patient to France to ensure that he learned all that he could to help her must be an amazing individual.

Within two weeks, Mike drove me back to Dr. West in San Francisco. I told him I would be having the surgery done by Dr. Connor.

"I am standing by my recommendation that you return to France for the surgery, Joanne," Dr. West said.

"I am never going back there, Dr. West. I know you are trying to help me, but I can't do it."

"Let me do some additional research. I know there is another team in France and I can send you there. The Egyptian physician who discovered PNE trained this team. You've got to go to surgeons who are more experienced. Dr. Connor is too new at it, and your case is complicated."

"After what happened to me, I won't consider going out of the country again. I am going to have Dr. Connor do the surgery."

Dr. West let out a huge sigh.

Kian and I left for the East Coast in late June. Using mileage upgrades, I flew first class again so I could lie on my side. Kian proved to be a great traveler and kept me entertained during the journey. Mike remained home so he could work, take care of the dog, and maintain our home. My mom, Bev, my brother David and his wife, Kris, flew to New Hampshire to support me during the month I'd be away.

The day arrived for my presurgical consultation and nerve latency tests. I dreaded both. Gathered in Dr. Connor's personal office, Mom, Patty, and Bev sat on a bench while I knelt on the floor, my customary pose for most office settings. We found Dr. Connor to be engaging, humorous, and caring. He was quick to smile, and the small creases around his bright eyes made me think he must enjoy laughing.

"I'm still relatively new in engaging with pudendal nerve patients, and I will never get used to speaking to them from a chair while they kneel on the floor," he said with embarrassment.

"You could kneel, too, and make it even weirder for your staff when they walk by," I teased.

He laughed easily and leaned forward in his chair.

"I know all of you are here to support Joanne and to make sure you have every question answered."

Bev spoke up first. "Dr. Connor, Jo told us that she is your eighteenth case. After the ordeal she suffered in France, we want to make sure there are no complications. What she went through in France was inhuman."

"Yes, I fully comprehend your concern. Let me show you exactly what's done during the surgery—maybe that will help with any other uncertainty." Dr. Connor got up and crossed the room to pick up a detailed structural model of the female pelvis. With the movement of the model, he showed us how the surgery would be conducted. This was the first time I had ever seen a three-dimensional view of what was wrong with my nerve canals.

"This is fascinating. I've only seen black-and-white pictures of the nerve canals and could never envision how they were compressed. This is a huge help. Thank you," I said.

My mom and sisters nodded. I could see the look of relief on their faces. Dr. Connor smiled, and before he could ask if we had any questions, my sisters interjected.

"What about pain control?" Bev asked.

"Yes, she can't suffer like she did in France," Patty added.

"I'm well aware of the lack of pain management in France, and there will be excellent care for you here, Joanne."

He continued to address us all. "I'll have you all speak to our anesthesiologist and you will have my cell number in case you have any questions during Joanne's recovery. I will order whatever amount of pain control medication she needs."

A wave of anxiety washed over me as a flashback of the fiasco in the French hospital filled my head. No matter how much I liked this doctor, I could not relax. I knew what was ahead for me. The nurse escorted my family to the waiting room while I was taken into an exam room for the dreaded test.

After Dr. Connor examined me, the nurse practitioner hooked me up to the electromyogram that would measure the nerve's response time. The clips were moved from my labia to my clitoris and anal cavity. Electric currents were run through them as they tested each area separately and then all together.

The pain for this test proved just as severe as it had always been. Flashes of painful memories shot through me like gunfire. I shook my head to try and dislodge the images, but they were impossible to suppress. My hands shook and my heart pounded as I clenched the sheet draped over me.

How much more, God? Help me! I can't do this alone. Frantic thoughts peppered my prayers.

The nurse practitioner looked at me from between my legs. "Try not to move, Joanne. I know this is uncomfortable."

"Uncomfortable is stubbing your toe. This is torture."

The nurse winced and moved more quickly.

"We just have to do the left side now, and then we'll be finished." Her voice was gentle, but I wondered if she had actually experienced the test firsthand. I was told she had learned how to administer the latency test from Dr. Vissar, Dr. Bedeau's partner.

I was sure that Dr. Vissar had never actually experienced the test himself, and I doubted this nurse practitioner had either.

The results of the test were staggering. Since September 2006 my right side had moved from a 7 (under 3 is normal) to more than 13. No wonder I was plagued with so much pain. My family and I met with Dr. Connor again to review the surgical plan and pain control measures based on the results of the latency test.

I would be admitted to the hospital the following day.

I was grateful Dr. Connor had given special permission for my mom to remain with me while I was in the pre-op area. When the anesthesiologist arrived to administer a spinal port, my mom held me while I cried. The surgical staff joked, smiled, and tried to do everything they could to make me feel safe. My eyes darted from one person to another. I heard their assurances, but I felt paralyzed.

Panic manifesting like static interference increased in my head. Their voices sounded as though they were far away—nothing was getting through. My mom rubbed my upper back above the spinal port while I shook and sobbed. *Please God, let this medication black me out! I can't get a grip. I'm coming unglued.*

Mercifully, blackout came.

When I woke in the recovery room it was evening. My legs were still numb from the epidural, and I noticed a controlled analgesia infusion pump (PCA) button my hand. I had used this before after other surgeries. The PCA allowed me to control the amount of pain medication I needed. My dread lessened as I experienced the relief of pain control.

The surgery was reported to have been successful with the nerve registering 3.3 with the latency test. Dr. Connor continued to give me full pain control measures for the days ahead. Seven days later, he discharged me from the hospital to Patty's home to recover.

※

My family surrounded me again. Their familiar love and care helped me heal. Kian kept busy in sailing camp and other amusing exploits with Patty and Mom, so I was free to completely rest. My medication levels moved to the highest they had ever been. I still had no appetite, but I was gaining hope.

Three weeks passed, and I finally felt strong enough to return home with Mom's help. Kian packed his backpack with the sailing knots he'd made in camp and wandered in to show me.

"Hey Mom, I'm gonna show these to Dad when I get home. Maybe we can go sailing sometime!"

"He's going to love all the work you did, sweetie. Wouldn't that be great if you guys could go sailing sometime?"

"Yeah, and maybe since they fixed your pain, you can come too." With that, he ran down the hallway to show my mom his backpack filled with treasures.

I won't be sailing or sitting for a long while, I thought. *God, let this surgery work. I know I'm in for another long recovery. I just need one good side to be able to offload pain. Thank You for hearing me and thank You for the love of my family.*

※

I felt excruciating pain every minute during the months of recovery—but then, something curious happened. A new symptom was added to my arsenal of agony. I felt like someone had lit a Fourth of July sparkler deep in my left butt cheek. The bizarre sensation occurred three or four minutes, four to five times a day. It felt like hundreds of ants marching to their anthill and launching fireworks as they moved. This strange symptom brought a greater need for extra pain control. After four days, the fire ended, and my usual pain cycle returned.

I continued to rise each morning before dawn, too afraid to think of what would happen to me if I stopped seeking God. In the guest room of our house, I would lie on my stomach on the floor with my Bible open in front of me, and I would cry out to the Lord for direction. I begged Him for mercy and healing, wisdom and peace.

I cried for my husband to be given back the healthy woman he had married. I prayed for my son to be given a pain-free mother who would be able to offer more patience and sympathy than I could now. I prayed for my mother and father, siblings, in-laws, and friends, that each would be delivered from the constant worry I caused them. I prayed for other people suffering with pudendal nerve entrapment.

I emerged from that room each morning with enough peace to face another day. Without that early-morning time with God, I could not function. Although I did not experience any definitive answers to my prayers, I knew that God had not forgotten His promise to me.

I memorized Scriptures to help me through the day. Praying these verses out loud brought the presence of the Holy Spirit and a way for me to connect deeply with the Lord. During the hardest days, I relied on 2 Corinthians 4:17–18 to bring perspective to my suffering:

> For our light and momentary troubles are achieving for us an eternal glory that far outweighs them all. So we fix our eyes not on what is seen, but on what is unseen, since what is seen is temporary, but what is unseen is eternal. (NIV)

Month after month, the bouts of brutalizing pain persisted, although the pattern wasn't consistent. Eventually, I began to experience a longer stretch of time between the huge pain flare-ups, particularly on my left side. This would be followed by the ants and fireworks sensation in my left buttock. I e-mailed Dr. Connor and asked him what he thought this meant.

Dr. Connor responded:

> Hi Joanne, This is a great sign that the left nerve is trying to regenerate. Nerve regeneration often feels like fire or heat moving rapidly across the injured nerve pathway. Try to remain patient. Nerves take a long time to regenerate, if they regenerate at all, but I'm hopeful that both your left and right sides will improve over time.

I kept his e-mail and read it for encouragement when I had particularly bad days. It was hard to remain patient.

⇒⇐

Three years following my surgeries in France, I finally experienced a partial regeneration of the pudendal nerve on my left side. I was grateful to God for any improvement, but I was especially glad that I could now offload weight from my still painful right side to my greatly improved left side. This development allowed me to slightly reduce the huge amount of pain medication I was taking. These small changes helped me find moments of peace in my body for the first time in a decade.

During this season, Mike did everything he could to support our family. Through it all he continued to amaze me. His dreams about intimacy in our marriage and our life together had been shattered just as mine had, yet he rarely spoke about them. Instead, he chose to help me through my suffering.

By 2009, I could stand or even sit with my special cushion, sometimes as long as fifteen minutes. This was a huge victory. It gave me more freedom, such as the ability to drive a little longer distance around town. It also allowed me to entertain the possibility of working a few hours a week. I yearned to ease some of the financial burden my husband had carried for so long.

I had befriended the administrative staff of the public charter school Kian attended. When the principal, Pat, heard of my improvement, she asked me to come to work for their growing multisite district.

"I would love to come and work with you, Pat, but I'm on a ton of narcotic pain meds still, and I can only sit for a max of fifteen minutes. How's that going to work?"

"Girl, I want you on this team. We need you in our human resources department. I know you and they know you. We all love you, and we'll make it work. You can work on the floor if you have to. We'll get you a special chair and whatever else you need."

"That's incredible. I don't know how it'll work but I'll try. I would love to be part of this group. When I'm struggling, I'll just come and lie on the floor of your office during one of your parent conferences," I said, as Pat snorted and walked away laughing.

After I had completed the formal interview process with the school's CFO, Melissa, I knew I was meant to work alongside her. We formed a deep friendship. The staff became family to me.

To do my job, I would kneel, lie on my stomach, squat, and walk—anything but sit. By the end of my workday, I would go home and collapse. I spent every weekend recouping on the couch and sitting in a scalding bath to be able to return to work on Monday. Some might argue that this wasn't much of a life; however, I felt blessed by God. For the first time in our family's history, we were finally able to live with some sense of routine and normalcy.

In God's perfect timing, Mike lost his job shortly after I started working. We obtained medical insurance through the school district, although not everything was covered by the plan—particularly my prescription medications. Just one of my four narcotic pain medications cost twelve hundred dollars a month.

Despite wondering how we would pay for my meds, we thanked God for my employment and for His impeccable provision.

22

Adversity and Discovery

Hardships often prepare ordinary people
for extraordinary destiny.

—C. S. LEWIS

Working and weekend recovery became the rhythm of my new life. My son and husband, once again, graciously adapted to my schedule and needs. Although we tried to hold on to some semblance of normalcy, we sacrificed other things that some might take for granted.

We rarely entertained at home, and we seldom went out. We developed the habit of rapidly eating every family meal so I could move around immediately afterward. We made the decision to return to church, but I paid a price for our attendance in increased pain—lying on my stomach or sitting on my knees with my blue cushion under my haunches, in the back of the sanctuary.

Despite my physical limitations, in 2010 I was asked to join the staff at our church as the executive administrator and assistant to the senior pastor. It sounded like a great opportunity for me to use my passion for God and His people in full-time ministry. Nevertheless, I hesitated to accept the offer.

Stepping down from my state job and into full-time ministry meant a significant reduction in salary, for which my family would bear the burden. It would also mean working on the weekends—not compatible with family life. My move into ministry would also disrupt the reliable pattern of pain management I had worked so hard to develop.

As I wrestled with these issues, I experienced a crisis of confidence. Would I be able to do what was required in the new role the church was creating for me?

My husband was extremely supportive, as we sought the Lord for confirmation of our decision. I discussed my concerns with the senior pastor several times—I wanted him to know exactly how limiting my physical abilities were. He assured me that he understood and was okay with all of it. Finally, with God's peace anointing the decision, I accepted the position.

As I moved into my new position at the church, pain management remained my biggest challenge. Despite the regeneration of much of the left pudendal nerve, the nerve damage on my right side continued to plague me. I relied on several types of opiate pain medications and a variety of ministrations, including scalding baths, squatting, kneeling, and lying down, to cope with the pain. My pain levels measured the days, months, and years for me. They were my compass, calendar, and clock. I longed to be free.

In 2012 I developed a different pain—this time in my right hip and pelvis. I now had more people praying for me than ever, so I was alarmed as the pain grew worse. I was not eager to undergo surgery again, and I tried every nonsurgical remedy prescribed or mentioned to me. Nothing worked. Diagnostic tests revealed multi-degenerative conditions in my right hip, which were due, most likely, to complications from my previous surgeries.

The doctors theorized that to compensate for the pudendal nerve pain, I had developed abnormalities in the way I stood and walked. These peculiar patterns, together with severe muscle weakness, changed my gait, stride, and the load on my legs, caus-ing my hip joint to no longer function correctly. Surgery was the only option.

Two separate surgeries were performed in 2013 to repair the damaged joint, and yet neither relieved my pain. Now I could no longer walk, sit, or stand without unrelenting pain. With this new development, coupled with my old, familiar pelvic nerve pain, I lost my battle with pain management and descended into despondency.

At the request of my physical therapist, my primary care physician appealed to my insurance company to send me to the best hip specialists in Northern California. The specialists called for more surgical intervention, but they could not give me any assurance that I would experience any significant improvement. Once again, I was trapped in a medical maze with no hope of escape.

Several good friends had gathered to form a prayer team to support me in my new job and to cover me in prayer through my latest hip issues. During one prayer meeting, a friend stood to release a word of prophecy she felt the Lord had given her a few minutes before. The scripture she shared sparked a rare glimmer of hope: "I have seen his ways, but I will heal him; I will lead him and restore comfort to him and to his mourners" (Isaiah 57:18 ESV).

After my visit to the hip specialists, the Lord prompted my friend Michelle to tell me there was a sense of urgency to pray more intensely for my healing. She directed the prayer team to aggressively pray for my healing. I was so glad they were fighting in prayer, because I had no fight left in me. With my affliction worse than ever, my thoughts were now tangled in a maze of their own.

I concluded that I had somehow brought this torture upon myself. I must have done something to displease God. I began habitually telling God how sorry I was for the vague, un-identifiable sin I knew I must have committed. I enjoyed a close relationship with Him, but hopelessness and fear had taken root in the deepest part of me.

Before the third hip surgery could be scheduled, my four-teenth surgery in fourteen years, it had to be approved by my insurance company. The approval process was slow, and the weeks dragged by with no news and no approval. In the midst of this, I received a revelation from God.

The revelation came as I was sent to a hip specialist from Stanford for a second opinion. Mike had to drive me to the San Francisco Bay Area because I could no longer sit long enough to drive myself. I was scheduled to meet with one of Stanford's leading orthopedic surgeons. It had taken months of work, negotiating the arduous process with my insurance company, to allow me to see an out-of-network doctor for a second opinion. The medical professionals in my area had run out of options, so, based on the reputation of this surgeon, I believed he possessed the only viable solution left for me to try.

I felt uneasy from the moment I arrived at his office. My pain levels were so high I thought I would vomit. After we waited for more than an hour, a nurse escorted me to an exam room. There I spent twenty minutes being interviewed by the resident doctor-in-training. Finally, the surgeon I came to see walked in.

I received a mere nod of the head as he launched into a dialogue with the resident doctor. As they spoke over me, I watched their interaction with keen interest. There was no mistaking the hierarchal order or the arrogance. The doctor's demeanor caused my heart to sink and brought flashbacks of the trauma I had experienced in France. I had waited months to see this man. Now, I could not process that I had believed this one man would be the answer to my prayers.

Help, Lord. Please let this doctor show some compassion, or get me out of here. I can't take anymore.

"Joanne." The doctor's voice startled me out of my thoughts—I was sure my shirt was moving up and down as war drums took the place of my heartbeat.

"Your case is very complex," he began. "Your history makes it impossible to know if the damage in the hip area is the reason for the pain. Twice you have had the area repaired, and you still have pain. You could undergo another surgery and not experience any relief. There isn't a simple solution here."

He was looking at my face as he spoke, but he avoided eye contact. There was a hint of scorn in his voice. I had experienced that look and tone from a surgeon years before who, despite my test results, felt my pain was in my head.

"I would like to do another surgery as long as you know there aren't any guarantees for improvement," he said as he walked out the door.

That was it. The nurse came in and gave me instructions for

filing the request for surgery with my insurance company. I felt like I had just received a blow to the head—there was buzzing in my ears and all the air left my chest at once.

Inside I ranted. *Another surgery is one more medical nightmare. I don't want this man touching me. How will I live with this pain? There is no way out of this. I can't do this, God. I can't do this anymore.*

I left the office, entered the elevator, and pressed the button. As I leaned up against the elevator wall, God spoke to me in an audible voice, "Contend for your healing!"

The loud and commanding words shook me, as did the way He said them. *What? What does it mean to contend for my healing?*

While Mike drove me back home that day, I asked the Holy Spirit to show me how to contend. I looked up the word *contend* on my smartphone. The definition "to pit oneself against" jumped out at me like a neon sign. *Yes, that's what I need to do, what God wants me to do. To pit myself against this diagnosis, the pain, the crumbling of my physical body, the emotional roller coaster of fear and anxiety, the discouraging words from medical professionals, the disappointment, the heartbreak, and devastation.*

I had to trust God again—to give it all over to Him and allow Him to fight for me, as I stood on His promises and not my experience. I hadn't realized until that very moment that I had almost given up on the fact that God heals. Now, with God's command to contend, I was shaken. I became fully aware that I must get back up and stand.

※

The next time I met with my prayer team, I shared my elevator experience and the revelation from God. They agreed to contend with me. We searched Scriptures to find the promises of God for healing. We began using them as warfare against the assault on my body. Living in constant pain caused intense physical exhaustion for me, but through the prayers of my friends, my spirit was renewed. I did not experience any physical relief, but my hope was now built on Christ's righteousness—with God's Word in my heart, I resolved not to give up for another day.

Months went by as I battled with my insurance company for approval of my next surgery. Despite having no guarantee for surgical success, I fought to have the surgery approved to provide myself with an option of potential help. I knew I could decline the surgery once approved, but to have no authorization meant I was left to contend without recourse. No other medical treatment or intervention was available through my own insurance network, and I could not imagine continuing to live with this level of pain and dysfunction.

As I geared up daily to contend against my mountain of misery, my thinking began to change. I always assumed we were supposed to pray for everyone, and then leave it up to God to heal or not. Now, however, I began to question whether God actually healed through prayer. For years people had prayed with me and for me, yet I felt no physical improvement. I prayed for healing with my prayer team, family, and friends, and still no advancement.

Having thirteen surgeries in fourteen years was extreme, and I began to question why the thousands of prayers lifted up during those years had not moved the heart of God to heal me. I wondered why the people I had prayed for had not experienced healing.

In all my years as a Christian, I had witnessed only one healing miracle. The miracle happened when our entire church prayed for a newborn baby with only one functioning lung. CAT scans showed a life-threatening disease in the second lung. After our church prayer, both lungs were clear, and subsequent CAT scans proved the presence of two healthy lungs.

The baby's miraculous healing made me keenly aware of the paradigm I had developed—pray for healing for each person, expect God to encourage each one, but do not expect physical or emotional healing to happen as a direct response. How did I come to believe that? I had great faith in the power of prayer, but discovered I had very little faith that God would heal someone right in front of me simply because I asked.

I researched healing ministries and discovered they existed all over the world. God was healing people, just not the people around me. The stories I read spoke of the power and authority given to each believer in Christ, enabling us to do the same things Jesus did in the power and authority of His name. When Jesus became my Lord and Savior, I was made into a new creation and given eternal life. I was also given His power and authority on the cross. I searched Scripture and found confirmation of this in Luke 10:19, Mark 16:18, and John 14:12.

With this revelation, I felt as though I was reading the Bible and understanding its truth for the first time. I was motivated to discover everything I could about healing through prayer. I read the gospel accounts of Jesus healing the sick. There He said we would heal the sick in His name. I studied the healing ministries of both classic and contemporary faith healers and read every book I could get my hands on concerning healing and deliverance and the believer's authority.

Bill Johnson's and Randy Clark's writings were particularly helpful to me as each included the biblical basis for healing and reinforced the truth of the Word of God and the powerful authority and identity of believers in Christ. I began to pray fervently that the Lord would use me to heal others and to teach them how to pray for the sick. I was tired of praying for people only to have nothing happen. I was loathsome of people praying for me with no results.

My paradigm was shifting.

23

Fire of God

*Miracles are a retelling in small letters of the very
same story which is written across the whole world
in letters too large for some of us to see.*

—C. S. LEWIS

In March 2013, during a time of deep prayer, I received a strong
directive from the Lord that I should go to a Christian healing
conference in Orlando, Florida. I had heard of healing conferences through the stacks of books and materials I had been
reading.

Dr. Randy Clark, well known for his healing ministry of
more than two decades, leads the Voice of the Apostles. Every
year this Christian organization holds an international conference on healing. This year's conference was in August, in
Orlando, Florida—but I couldn't imagine going. I simply could
not make a journey like that with my current pain levels. Sitting

on an airplane for five and a half hours would be impossible for me.

Lord, why do I need to go to this conference? You can teach me what I need to know right here.

I heard, "Just go. You'll be blessed."

I knew I had heard clearly, so now I had a decision to make. I called my best friend, Michelle, and asked if she'd accompany me to the conference. She had been waiting to travel with me for fourteen years. Throughout my health ordeal, Michelle had always believed that God would heal me. She was so convinced of it that she had saved her frequent flyer miles with the goal of taking me to Greece after I was healed.

Seeing the Greek islands had been a dream of mine. In 2008, after years of waiting for healing to happen, those frequent flyer miles expired. While Greece remained an unattainable goal for me, Michelle was thrilled when I laid out for her the impression from God that I should go to Orlando.

"We are going! Something is going to happen there. Maybe God's going to heal you."

I didn't want to get my hopes up and had little faith for my own healing; I just wanted to learn more about healing ministry. Still, I thought a lot about what she said. We made our travel plans, and I tried to ignore my pain.

The August departure date arrived, and another friend, Monica, joined us on the journey. Despite the pain in my body, an unusual peace settled over me and snuffed out even the tiniest spark of fear. *I know this is You, Lord.*

On Monday morning, we boarded the plane and headed straight for the exit row where I could stretch out my legs while slouched in my seat. The exit row was staggered and a single seat nearest the exit door offset the row of seats we chose.

"You know, I really shouldn't sit in an exit row since I can't perform the functions of pushing out the door, inflating a slide and a raft, and all the other stuff you have to do if we crash. I would faint if I had to blow out birthday candles. I have no stomach muscles left."

Monica laughed. "We'll cover for you, Jo. I have some serious lungs."

Michelle leaned forward to look at me. "Do you have your cushion under you?"

"Yeah, but it's not enough. I can't turn my body enough to take the pressure off. I need God to do something here if I am going to make it five hours."

Within minutes, the gentleman with the solo seat next to the exit door overheard our conversation and asked if I would like his seat. I couldn't believe it! His seat had no seat in front or beside it, so I could sit in a way that would take the pressure off my pelvis and hip. With my new seat assignment and the handful of narcotics I took to control my pain, I made it to Orlando.

The rental car was tiny and did not allow me the room I needed to manage my pain effectively. The ride to our condo had me squirming all over the back seat trying to shake the pain, but the pitch of the seats made it impossible. I swallowed hard at my rising pain levels and chose to focus instead on God—after all, He had given me provisions, strength, and enough meds to make it across the country. When we arrived at the condo parking lot, I wanted to simply lie down on the blacktop; sleep could not come soon enough.

⋙⋘

The next morning, Michelle, Monica, and I entered the convention center designed to hold ten thousand people. Immediately, we could feel a change in the atmosphere. Worship music was already playing, and the presence of the Lord was palpable. We walked into what some call "an open heaven," the place where you can literally feel the presence of God. It's as if all natural laws are temporarily suspended, and heaven simply breaks in with signs and wonders, miracles and healing, revelations and manifestations of power.

Before we left California, during a time of intense prayer in preparation for traveling, the Lord had shown me a brief overhead view of this room. Now, as I stood in the main hall, I was amazed at how precise the vision had been. He also had shown me exactly where we were to sit—in the twelfth or thirteenth row from the front on the left side facing the stage.

Because the room was already filling up, there did not appear to be enough seats in the rows God had designated. I turned to go toward the back of the room where there were plenty of empty seats.

Monica spoke up. "Hey, didn't God say we needed to sit in those rows?"

"Yeah, He did. He told Jo we were supposed to sit there," Michelle said.

I kept my distance as my two tenacious friends walked up to the man occupying the aisle seat in the thirteenth row.

"Excuse me, but God told my friend we are supposed to sit in this row," they said almost in unison, pointing to me as I clutched my blue cushion in my hands.

The man and his friend next to him jumped up simultaneously and yelled down the row of about thirty-five people.

"Hey, y'all, move down. God told these girls they're supposed to sit here."

My mouth fell open as I watched an entire row of people

cheerfully get up and shift around until three seats opened right in the middle of the row—just as I had seen in the vision God had given me.

Okay, Lord. You are amazing.

"That was crazy," I said aloud to Monica and Michelle as we scooted into the row.

We were all laughing. The people around us were delighted that we were seated where the Lord had told us to sit. We engaged in conversation with those nearest us. I was concerned, as usual, about my ability to sit for any length of time—but I knew if God had cleared this row for us, He would certainly help me deal with my pain. Something within my spirit began to shift.

I had received occasional prophetic words from the Lord for people or about people throughout my Christian walk, but, under this open heaven, I was about to experience a whole new level. Before the event officially kicked off, I felt compelled to pray for the couple to our left. Michelle and I laid our hands on the shoulder of the husband. He was a pastor by the name of Keith. Out of my mouth poured an avalanche of prophecy and blessing of astonishing detail and specificity.

I had never seen this man before in my life, and the things coming out of my mouth stunned me. Keith and his wife were overcome with emotion, and their eyes were wide in wonder at what the Holy Spirit had done. Michelle and I were astounded right along with them.

"Are y'all with them?" Keith said, pointing to the conference stage.

We laughed hard.

"No, we're here to learn. I have no idea what happened just now," I replied.

"Well, maybe you ought to be with them," he said, laughing

and crying at the same time. "Everything you said was exactly what's going on with us and our church. You even brought up the things we've been dreaming about doing. Man, I don't even know what just happened, but God is good."

Michelle turned and looked at me, and we cracked up. That is how it went all week long. People would come up to me and say things such as, "I feel drawn to you. Would you pray for me?" Michelle would grab my purse and my pillow, Monica would turn on her cell phone's voice recorder, I would lay my hand on the person, and then the Holy Spirit would download encouragement through me to these beautiful people.

I had never felt so close to the Lord. I was experiencing His love for people in such a new and profound way. I was moved to tears and laughter, over and over again.

God blessed me with many moments of prayer and impartation throughout the week. On a few occasions the presence of the Holy Spirit so overpowered me that I was catapulted to the floor and felt as if I were being electrocuted as wave after wave of power jolted my body. I saw things in the heavens that overwhelmed me—heavenly hosts and the glory of God. I heard the Lord tell me things that were intensely personal and amazing. I was stunned by His love and laid out by His power.

One afternoon, I stayed on the floor in a prostrate state for such a long time that Michelle, Monica, and some new friends we had made, left me there and went on to attend the afternoon classes in another part of the conference center. When I was finally able to get off the floor, I prophesied over a pastor, an evangelist, and an ice cream server. The guy scooping ice cream said, "I don't know who you people are, but I hope I'm here next year when y'all come back. Just today, I've had nine of you tell me everything about my life and where God is calling me."

I was having an absolute blast. I likened the conference to being in God's Disneyland. Throughout the conference, I received prayer from incredible believers and saw others physically healed by the power of the Holy Spirit. Through those experiences I was stretched and blessed, but I was not healed.

⁂

God clearly had amazing things in store for me at this conference, but healing was evidently not one of them. Although I felt such joy at being caught up in what God was doing supernaturally, my pain kept pulling me back to my physical reality. The intimacy with Jesus that I experienced was so profound that I determined to keep my focus on Him and do my best to ignore the pain that vied for my attention.

That week I attended a class to learn how to hear the Holy Spirit better. I picked up a practice from the instructor that I still use today—asking the Holy Spirit for the word for that day. On the morning of the last day of the conference, Friday, August 16, I asked the Holy Spirit for the word for the day. I heard Him say my word was *happy*.

During the week we had collected a variety of new friends. Our new tribe hailed from South Africa, New Zealand, and Washington, DC. We'd been praying, sharing, and laughing together the whole week, and it felt as if we were now family. Gene and David were part of this tribe and had been the first to pray for me on the opening night of the conference.

Here were two guys from opposite ends of the world—Gene, from Washington, DC, with his doctorate in Information Technology, and David, a rabbit shooter from New Zealand. I marveled to think that by worldly standards these two wouldn't have much in common, but in God's kingdom what you do for a living is not a factor. Gene and David were bonded as brothers by the extravagant love of God and the assurance that the Father's will was to heal everyone. They were on a mission to fulfill the words of Jesus in Matthew 10:8—to heal the sick, cast out demons, and raise the dead.

Even though I was not healed when they prayed for me the first night, I was fascinated by what they said and how they prayed. I wanted to pray with that kind of faith. The more I got to know these men, the more my faith grew for other people to be healed. On the other hand, my faith for my own healing did not grow.

"You know, Jo, we aren't going to leave this place tonight until you get healed," Gene said matter-of-factly on the last night of the conference.

I raised my eyebrows in wonder at his confidence.

"That's it. We're going to stay all night and pray if we have to. You can't go home in this pain. It's not right," David added.

I was overwhelmed by the love these two had for all the people they prayed for, including Michelle, Monica, and me. The love of Jesus emanated from them—far beyond human love or compassion. Gene and David carried the presence of the living God. I appreciated their confidence, but I did not share their belief that I would be healed. I didn't want to get my hopes up only to have them dashed once more.

I had always thought I had faith to believe I would be healed, but when healing didn't come for so long, I concluded it was because I was not worthy. I came to believe God wouldn't do anything to decrease my pain, because I simply couldn't be trusted to pursue a godly life without pain as a compass.

"You guys are amazing. I so appreciate your support, love,

and prayers, but I have an early flight in the morning, and I don't think they'll let us camp in this building all night," I said, hoping my response would hide my discouragement.

Protests rose from everyone in our group. David came over to wrap me in a hug.

"I just think something's going to happen tonight," Michelle said.

Our South African friend, Lollie, walked over to join the David hug. "Yeah, Jo, we are going to pray until God comes. I don't want you to suffer anymore."

Monica and Gene nodded in agreement. Gene stood in the aisle praying. He was determined. His mother-in-law also came by and joined our circle of prayer warriors.

I got so choked up I couldn't respond. I remained in the hug huddle until a wave of that familiar pain sent me back to the floor on my knees where I prayed: *Incredible, Lord! They are absolutely sure that You want to heal me. They believe You want to heal me now. Their faith is amazing. Please bless them, answer their prayers, and cover their families with safety.*

I remained on the floor in my kneeling position. Worship in the hall was winding down, as the conference drew to a close. There was a call from the podium for anyone who had been healed to come forward. With almost seven thousand people in attendance, a virtual sea of people surged up to the stage.

Monica had received an amazing healing in her body for orthopedic conditions, including flat feet. Just the day before we watched the miracle unfold before us as her feet formed arches under the power of the Holy Spirit. Michelle's chronic neck pain, from a car accident that had happened seventeen years before, also disappeared. Monica headed up to the stage to offer her testimony, giving God all the glory for what He had done for her.

With only two hours left before the close of the conference, I remained deep in prayer and worship, thanking Him for the love and powerful revelation that He'd given me that week about my identity as His beloved child. When I opened my eyes, I watched as a man dressed in a black shirt and black pants approached me. He was in his late sixties or early seventies, with a thick, white hair and a big, gentle smile.

"What's your story?" he asked, with the strongest Texas drawl I had ever heard.

I looked up to meet his eyes, as my pain level began to increase. So many people had prayed for my healing by this point in the conference that I was weary of telling my whole story. I figured I could give this man the one-minute version of my health woes and be done with it—he'd move on and I could go back to praying.

"I've had chronic, debilitating pain from nerve damage for fourteen years and have been through thirteen surgeries. I'm facing another surgery when I return home."

"Can I pray for you?" he said, with a compassionate but intense look.

"Sure, thanks," I replied without a tinge of faith in my voice.

I immediately became aware of how awkward I felt on my knees before this man, speaking at the same level as his crotch, so I stood up. I used my hands to push myself off the floor to a standing position while he waited.

The man took one of my hands in his and prayed a simple prayer. When he did this, the power of God came upon me, so forcefully that I fell backward. Michelle and our other friends lowered me to the ground. The man left, but I remained on the ground for about fifteen minutes.

I was aware of the presence of the Holy Spirit coursing

through me with the same power and intensity I had felt during other encounters with God during the week. Wave after wave of the love of Jesus pulsed through my body. When the intensity of that encounter began to subside and I could sit up, I looked into the eager faces of Michelle, Gene, David, and Lollie.

"Are you healed?" "Is your pain gone?" "That was wild!" "This is it!" "This has got to be the one!" Their faith was palpable.

"I'm the same, but it's okay. I've been this way for such a long time."

David began to cry again. He'd prayed over me earlier in the evening for almost an hour, and despite his beautiful intercession I had not been healed. Michelle declared again that she believed I would be healed that night.

"Your testimony is way more powerful if you're healed tonight than if you stay this way," she reasoned.

I felt another huge rush of gratitude for their faith, but it did not change my lack of faith.

I moved back to my knees and waited for Monica to go up on the stage to testify to her healing. I looked up to see the man in black coming toward me again. This time I could see his name tag clearly. His name was Richard.

"How are ya?" he drawled.

I wanted to roll my eyes at the thought of enduring another prayer session during which I wasn't going to be healed. Instead, I tried to politely brush him off.

"Oh, Richard," I said, "I'm the same, but it's okay because I've been this way such a long time and it's—"

Before I could finish my sentence, Richard cut me off and yelled, "*No!* God healed me! He healed my wife! He healed my son! And now He's gonna heal you!"

Whoa! It felt like the force of his words parted my hair. I

didn't know how to respond, so I nodded my head in stunned agreement. This guy was intense!

Then Richard quietly asked if he could sit in the empty chair next to me. I nodded again, shocked as much by the abrupt change in his demeanor as by his unwavering confidence that God would heal me.

Richard took my face between his hands and held it in a tight clasp. Looking at me with loving, compassionate eyes, he instructed me not to break eye contact with him. I sensed that I was looking into the eyes of Jesus. Then he spoke.

Richard had me renounce my agreement with the spirit of death and suicide, unworthiness, guilt, shame, rejection, and so many other things. He led me through the repentance of the vows and beliefs I held that God wanted me ill all these years as a way of teaching me. Richard told me I was forgiven for everything I had ever done. He pronounced all power of the Enemy to harm me broken in the name of Jesus.

He then began to speak healing over every single thing that was wrong with my body, including thyroid disease, food allergies, esophagus issues, and other ailments that had come on me during the past few years. Some of the illnesses he called out I had never told anyone about. I had not even shared a few of them with my own husband because I was so sick of burdening him with my health issues.

I sobbed uncontrollably. Michelle, who was sitting next to me, leaned over to me and whispered in my ear, "Who is this guy? Do you think he's an angel?"

She said exactly what I was thinking, but I couldn't answer her. I was shaking uncontrollably under the power of the Holy Spirit.

Richard grinned from ear to ear and giggled a little. "Is it all right if I pray for your private parts?"

Are you kidding? I nearly laughed aloud at the absurdity of the question. Richard was familiar with more of the intimate details of my life than anyone I knew. I was not going to throw up a roadblock now. I felt like a ten-ton truck had been lifted off me already, and I was ready for the rest to leave.

I nodded in response to his question, while the rest of my body shook and trembled under the weight of the Holy Spirit.

"All right then . . . Michelle, you put your hand here," pointing to the lowest part of my abdomen, "and I'll put one finger on top of your hand. That all right with you?"

I nodded again, feeling like a bobble-head doll on a dashboard.

Richard then commanded all the pain, imbalances, inflammation, and misalignment to be healed in Jesus' name. Immediately, I felt the pain that I had lived with for more than fourteen years lift off me.

I was in shock. I wobbled around. I could not process the fact that I had no pain. I cried even harder, right along with Michelle, who by now was practically in my lap!

Richard couldn't smile any bigger. "All right, then! Get up and do something you couldn't do."

With Richard and Michelle on either side of me to keep me from toppling over, I placed my right foot in front of me and prepared to stand. I had been unable to bring my right foot around to the front of me for four years because of my deteriorating hip and pelvic instability.

When my foot came forward with ease and without pain, my shock only increased. With Michelle and Richard steadying me, I kicked my right leg high into the air, a maneuver I had not been able to do in years. *This is insane!*

I was simultaneously laughing and crying now as a thought

flew in my head. *I am going to be one of those crazy healed people running up and down the aisles at this conference!* In my self-pity and discouragement, those exuberant, newly healed people had annoyed me all week.

Richard said, "Why y'all crying? Aren't y'all happy?"

Happy. There it was—my word for the day. *God, You are amazing!*

Richard interrupted my thoughts. "Come on, you gotta go up there on stage and give God the glory for this."

I had flippers for feet and could hardly stand, but Richard and Michelle walked me toward the front to the stage. We had been far in the back of the ten-thousand-person conference hall, so this was a hike, one I would not have been able to do earlier without increased pain. As soon as the security team manning the metal barricades in front of the stage saw Richard coming toward them, the gates opened up like it was Moses parting the Red Sea.

Once more, Michelle spoke close to my ear. "Who is this guy? He must be someone important."

I was smiling but couldn't form a coherent sentence. I was focused on getting up on that stage to give glory to God.

Just then, Monica saw us coming up the aisle. She had been standing in line to give her testimony but ran over to us. "What? Are you kidding?! Did you get healed?! Like all-the-way healed?!"

Michelle and I nodded yes through our tears.

Richard laughed and turned to Michelle. "Y'all got it from here? You might have to talk for her and tell the story." Then he walked away.

The only thing we knew about him was that his name was Richard, but we saw him enter the second row in the center section of the auditorium.

Michelle announced, "He's gotta be with Global Awakening, Jo. Only friends and family or ministry partners sit this close to the front."

I filed her comment away, but I was too overcome with joy to process anything.

Just before I gave my testimony on stage, one of the organization's leaders, Paul Martini, came up to me and asked what had happened. Filled to overflowing with the Holy Spirit's presence, I found I couldn't answer. Michelle and Monica stepped in to tell him about my miraculous healing while I stood between them, grinning and shaking with joy. I was overwhelmed by the thought that Jesus had just healed me—completely.

"This is wonderful! Praise God! Wow! Okay, as soon as the lady in green finishes giving her testimony, you will go up next. Just tell everyone what happened as briefly as you can. Our whole goal here is to give God all the praise and glory. Randy might ask you some specific questions about your healing, but he doesn't always. Okay?"

I was so giddy, so shocked, I'm not sure I gave any sort of intelligible answer.

By the time it was my turn to approach the microphone, I had some of my mental faculties back, but my hands were flailing as if I were trying to flag down a cab. Laughing, Paul said he would hold the microphone for me.

Through fresh tears, and with my voice breaking, I spoke. "I feel like I just got hit by lightning! I have been in hell for fourteen years suffering in pain. I've had thirteen surgeries, and I was told I need another. For such a long time I believed the lie that God didn't want to heal me. I agreed with the Enemy that God could only use me in my pain."

I exhorted everyone to believe God was willing and desired

to heal. I told them not to listen to the Enemy. For the first time, I publicly communicated my silent belief system. I confessed to thousands of people that I had believed a falsehood about God—that my own will was so rebellious and untrustworthy that God had caused me to physically deteriorate in order that my will would conform to His. I had not fully understood that Christ died for my sin and rebelliousness to restore me to the love of the Father. Instead, I had believed pain was God's way of teaching me and keeping me in line. I divulged my underestimation of Satan's power to oppress me, sharing that I had unknowingly given him that right all these years.

When I encouraged the room full of faith-filled children of God to believe it was the will of God to heal them, the entire room stood to its feet. Together we gave God glory with shouts of praise and clapping. Pain had consumed me twenty-four hours a day, seven days a week, for more than fourteen years—and now it was gone. What joy! What peace! What an amazing Lord and King!

❊

Later that night we found Richard again, and he told me that the first time he prayed for me he had been on his way to the restroom. Along the way, the Holy Spirit spoke to him and told him to pray for my healing. After Richard prayed for me, he continued on to the restroom and then returned to his seat next to his wife. As soon as he sat down, the Lord told him to get up and go back to me a second time. He did—and his obedience changed my life.

At the close of the conference, after almost everyone had left, I ran up and down the aisles of the meeting room. I kicked up my right leg and danced around in celebration of what God had done. I hadn't been able to do so many things with my body for so many years that I wanted to do all those things in one night. I laughed and cried throughout the night. I prayed for anyone who asked. Our little tribe of friends stayed on to pray for others until 3:30 a.m.

The Lord had moved powerfully in me, and I could now imagine a life I never thought I would have: a life of pain-free freedom and supernatural blessing. The things I had thought were impossible were now within reach. When we returned to the condo that morning to pack for our flight home, I threw away the blue pillow that had accompanied my rear end for the past ten years. I could not stop smiling.

At the time of my miraculous healing, I was taking seven different medications, including heavy narcotics like OxyContin, Norco, and Ultracet, as well as medication for autoimmune thyroid disease, hormone replacement, prescription sleeping pills, and prescription laxatives. Although I don't advocate this action to anyone else, I stopped taking all seven medications that night.

Just before I dumped the pills into the commode, I recalled a conversation I had with my pain management doctor in 2008.

"If you ever have a surgery that eliminates the pain, Joanne, you'll need to be hospitalized for some time to manage the withdrawal from all your medications. Because of the combination of drugs and the dependence your body has developed, controlled withdrawal from the opiates and sleeping pills is the only way to prevent serious side effects."

The presence of the Lord had created such a level of trust and peace in me that I knew He had healed me of this as well. I didn't have any withdrawal symptoms then or thereafter.

※

I attempted to pack my suitcase, but I couldn't stop wandering around the condo praising God. We had a plane to catch in two hours. Peace and the incredible closeness of the Holy Spirit engulfed me while I tried to comprehend what had happened to me. What a miracle God! Out of His extravagant love He set up the entire thing so His daughter could be set free.

The next day Michelle was reading Randy Clark's biography and discovered our Richard was Richard Holcomb—the man who gave the prophetic word to Randy Clark in 1994 about going to Toronto, Canada, where he had a central role in the Toronto Revival. Randy's worldwide healing ministry began from that time in Toronto. Richard had traveled the world in healing ministry with Randy and for more than thirty years had been one of Randy's foremost intercessors.

God healed me through the willingness and faith of Richard Holcomb, by the blood of Jesus, and by the power of the Holy Spirit. This brother in Christ, who lived the command of Jesus in Matthew 10:8, blessed me with its words: "Heal the sick, raise the dead, cleanse the lepers, cast out demons. Freely you received, freely give" (NASB).

I am forever grateful for this godly, obedient man but most of all for the amazing love and power of Jesus Christ.

※

The next year, in celebration of my healing, I went once again to the Voice of the Apostles conference. I prayed that the Lord would allow me to run into Richard Holcomb there.

The afternoon before the conference started I was in the

upper lobby of the Orlando Convention Center, about to attend a partner luncheon for Global Awakening. As I walked toward the banquet room, I heard a familiar voice.

"Hey, hey!"

I turned around to see Richard standing there with his arms open. I ran into his embrace and burst into tears. He held my head against his shoulder and cried right along with me.

"You and I are bonded together forever because of what the Lord did for you."

I could only nod in response as gratitude overwhelmed my heart. The Lord healed me, but what Richard did for me reminded me of a teaching by Heidi Baker called "Stop for the One."

In that lesson, she explains that we need to stop for the person in front of us—to be the light of Christ for that person; to do what the Holy Spirit leads us to do; to say what He tells us to say; and to spread the love of Jesus to that one person. We should make a difference in that one life because that is what we are called to do as believers in Christ. I was grateful for the opportunity to thank Richard for stopping for me and altering my life forever.

Richard and I marveled at the love and power of God and were joined in our rejoicing by Michelle and our fellow travelers. When we released our embrace, I looked at Richard, who was wiping his nose, and said, "I don't know how to thank you. You have no idea how different my life is now. I've taken my son to amusement parks to ride roller coasters because I can! My husband and I have a life together again. I've hiked the national parks in New Mexico with my sisters! I'm working out again and I feel great! But the best part is, I am seeing God do miracles and heal people when I pray."

My lip quivered as fresh tears flowed.

"I believe the angels in heaven are rejoicing right now because we are here in this moment together celebrating what God has done," Richard said.

I could only nod silently as we walked arm in arm into the banquet room.

Afterword

Do you think the pain will come back?" Mike said, still in shock after I relayed my healing story.

"No. Richard told me that if the pain started to feel like it wanted to return, I just had to say, 'No! Get out in the name of Jesus!'"

Mike was afraid to hope, but he couldn't deny what he saw— his wife moving, standing, and walking without pain. The fact that I could sit for extended periods of time, and without a cushion, meant I was again the woman he knew before our son was born. For weeks after my healing, Mike continued to ask if I had pain. I finally asked him to stop because I no longer wanted to focus on pain but on life.

The return of our intimacy offered another major confirmation to us that God was indeed redeeming all the years the Enemy had robbed from us.

Kian sat with his mouth open when I told him the story of how God had healed me. I loved every minute of sharing with him my experience with the miraculous, healing power of Jesus.

"So all of your pain is gone?" he asked, while I nodded and smiled. "That's just crazy. How's that possible?"

"God is huge, Kian. Way bigger than we can understand."

I went on to tell him about the lies Satan uses to keep us sick and trapped, and how we must not come into agreement with his deception. What we come into agreement with has power over us. We need to be united with God's Word and what He says about us, through His Son, Jesus.

I think I lost him halfway through my explanation, when he asked me about more important things. "Okay, so does that mean we can go to Universal Studios and you can ride roller coasters with me?" he said.

"Yep. We will do that in celebration. How's that?"

"That's awesome. Tell me when!" He hugged me tight and ran out the door with his skateboard in tow.

My physical therapist and prayer-warrior friend, Tiffany, was the next person I told. I thought I'd have a little fun, so I didn't tell her of my healing at the beginning of our therapy session.

"What happened to you? Nothing feels the same!" she said as she manipulated my lower body, just as she had done every Wednesday for a year and a half. I laughed at her confusion.

Tiffany burst into tears. "Oh, my gosh! You got healed!"

I cried in response and told her what happened. She began maneuvering my body in ways it never could move before. She measured my ranges of motion and strength, and found that my right leg was now stronger and more flexible than my left.

Tiffany prepared a report on my status. I took her amazing findings to my primary care doctor later that week. Although he could not explain my sudden absence of pain or the increased strength and flexibility I demonstrated, he refused to believe that God had healed me. Instead he attributed my healing to the power of the brain. I couldn't help but roll my eyes.

"If God wasn't responsible for my healing, how is it possible that I no longer need my pain medication?" He swiveled his stool to face me head on with eyebrows raised.

"Doesn't it seem incredulous that I didn't need to be admitted to the hospital to get off the narcotic medications after more than a decade?

He was stunned. "When did you stop taking medication?"

"The night I was healed by God."

"You stopped cold turkey? OxyContin, Norco, Ultracet, and Klonopin?"

"Yep." I nodded. "And don't forget the thyroid meds, hormone patches, and the one for acid reflux."

"I'm not sure how you could do that."

I leaned forward and locked eyes with him. "When I received prayer for healing, there was a power that came on me and ran through my whole body like high intensity electricity. It was fiery, and it caused me to shake all over for a long time. As the person prayed in the name of Jesus, the intensity got stronger and stronger. When the prayer was over, I didn't have any more pain."

Silence.

Clearing his throat, Dr. Wong said, "Wow. That's weird."

I pressed on before he could say something else. "I came

here to see if you would please send me to get another 3-D CT scan, so we can see the before and after of my pelvis and hip problems. I'd like to send documented proof of my healing to Global Awakening."

"You have an HMO insurance policy, and they won't approve another scan since you just had one a month ago. It's too expensive," he said, studying my chart again. Then he looked back to me. "I'm glad you don't have pain anymore, Joanne. We don't know why the brain does what it does, but it sounds like yours created a new pathway due to some sort of current. I saw that in medical school when one of my classmates had electro acupuncture. His pain came back a few days later."

"Well, that was acupuncture, and this was the Holy Spirit. My pain won't return. Ever."

He didn't respond as I got off the table. I thanked him for his time and walked out the door.

Lord, please help him to see that You are the ultimate healer and that You can choose any way You want to bring a body to wholeness.

As I drove home, I thought of my doctor and his lack of faith. He was not a believer in Christ, yet his lack of faith was not much different than my own during my fourteen-year battle with pain. Despite being a believer in Christ, I didn't have much more faith for my own healing than my doctor had. I was just beginning to discover what I had been given through Christ's death and resurrection.

Yes, I thought, *this is the victorious life I didn't know was possible until I experienced my healing transformation.* The cross of Christ allows me to scorn shame and sin. The Enemy tried to get me to agree with sin and shame, but now, because I knew the truth, he could not take me down again.

I said *"No!"* to any pain I experienced during the first two weeks following my healing. Each time, the pain instantly disappeared. After two weeks of remaining steadfast, any pain trying to return vanished. There were no more attempts from the Enemy to lure me into doubting that God healed me 100 percent.

"Submit to God. Resist the devil, and he will flee from you" (James 4:7 NIV). I resisted the devil and he vanished, just as the Bible said he would.

※

All I wanted to do was take the Father's hand and let Him work through me to bring His freedom to others. I had been moved from merely having the knowledge of who God is, to having an experience with God and a vibrant, heart-to-heart love affair with Jesus Christ through the power of His Holy Spirit.

Instead of looking at myself as Christ's indentured servant, I began looking at Him as my beloved friend. He was Lord, but He was also the friend dearest to my heart. I was giddy with excitement to see others receive healing from God. Following the Holy Spirit is an adventure.

To partner with God in His desire to heal others involves being willing to step out in faith, even when it's uncomfortable. My faith risks started on the way home from the conference where I was healed. I prayed and prophesied over the airline mechanic in the seat next to me as I flew home. I had been given impressions from the Lord before the conversation between the mechanic and I ever took place—specifics about the man's daughters, a separation with his wife, the resentment eating a hole in his heart. I decided if Richard was obedient to the Lord and I was healed, I could step out in faith and ask the Lord to touch this man.

"So, do you live in Florida?"

"No, I'm just here for a short vacation." He was hung over and wearing sunglasses.

"Do you mind if I share something with you?" I asked as I turned in my seat to face him.

He didn't appear amused. "Yeah, okay. I guess, but I really need to sleep. I was up having a little too much fun last night."

"Awesome. I'll make it quick," I said.

I shared the things God had showed me about him in an encouraging way.

He leaned forward, popped the shades up onto his head and stared at me. "That's nuts. How do you know all that stuff?"

"I'm sure you'll think this is weird, but sometimes God shows me things to help people know He loves them." *There. I said it.*

The mechanic pushed his shades down over his eyes and leaned back, facing forward against his seat. He started talking.

"So, my two daughters are on this flight a few rows behind me. One is a dancer and the other an artist, just like you said. Both are having a really tough time with their mom and me splitting. I'm off the deep end, spun out by what my wife did. I have so much resentment I feel like my stomach is on fire all the time. I want to relocate here to Florida, just like you talked about, but I don't know how to do that because we have split custody."

While he took a breath, I felt the Lord nudge me to listen to more of his story.

"Would you like to talk about it?" I asked.

"I guess. All we have is time, right?" he said while I nodded.

As I listened to his story of betrayal and heartbreak, I asked the Lord how I should respond to him. I didn't get any prompting to preach to him or to try and sell him on Jesus. What I felt was an overwhelming sense of God's love for His broken child.

"Would you be cool with me praying for you? I keep my eyes open when I pray. It'll be quiet and I promise not to be bizarre."

We both laughed.

"I guess, since you already knew everything, it's okay if you pray, but I don't do religion. My name is Mark."

"That's great, Mark, because I'm not religious."

The Lord's kindness and love for Mark was unmistakable. Throughout my prayer, the Holy Spirit revealed more details of his life, including childhood trauma. Tears streamed down from under the frames of his sunglasses as He felt the Lord's presence. He chose to forgive his wife.

"Wow! I don't feel my gut burning anymore. I drank a half bottle of Jack last night and I feel great. My headache's gone too. I don't get what's happening here, but man, I'm glad I sat next to you."

"When you get off the plane, you can tell your friends that you met a crazy lady who hears from God, and God sent her to tell you how much He loves you," I said.

"That was the wildest conversation I have ever had in my life. Thank you," he said.

I laughed and told him to remember about the job and relocation, and things about his daughters' futures that were prophesied over him. He smiled and nodded.

Down in the baggage claim area he pointed to his daughters, collected his bags, and gave me one more "thumbs up" at the exit door.

You're amazing, God.

⋇

Since then, my boldness and confidence has grown. I completed all the coursework in Global Awakening's Christian Healing

Certification Program to learn all I could about doing what Jesus did. I have given my testimony in many venues, preached and taught, trained prayer teams, and brought these teams to churches all over the world.

I have traveled with Global Awakening several times as a member of a prayer team, where I saw the Lord heal more than three thousand people in one week. I have witnessed as people with stage IV cancer were healed—with clear PET scans to prove it.

I have prophesied over, prayed for, and trained hundreds of people seeking to be used by God to bring His healing power to the sick. They report dramatic healings of people with cancer and other chronic or fatal illnesses as they pray by the power of the Holy Spirit and in the name of Jesus.

Blind eyes are opened, deaf ears hear, and the lame walk. I have seen God's healing break out in my church—a church that had previously experienced only one miraculous healing in its seventeen years.

The prayer team in our church of five thousand people grew from three people to more than fifty-five in the months following my return from Florida. Most of the prayer team members felt a call to join in healing others by the power of Jesus after God radically healed them of their personal afflictions. They now want to freely give away what they have been given—committed to seeing others healed and set free from the lies of the Enemy, giving all the glory to God.

This is the divine life; this is the life Jesus died for us to find. This is the kingdom of God brought to earth—the pearl of great price.

Paul wrote: "The only thing that counts is faith expressing itself through love" (Galatians 5:6 NIV).

It is only through the love of Jesus that we operate in His

power and authority.: "And [Jesus] called to him his twelve disciples and gave them authority over unclean spirits, to cast them out, and to heal every disease and every affliction" (Matthew 10:1 ESV).

Jesus didn't tell us to pray for the sick. His command is to heal the sick, raise the dead, cleanse lepers, cast out demons. "You received without paying; give without pay" (Matthew 10:8 ESV). Then Jesus sent out six dozen more disciples. "After this the Lord appointed seventy-two others and sent them on ahead of him, two by two, into every town and place where he himself was about to go" (Luke 10:1 ESV).

And He said to them, "The harvest is plentiful, but the laborers are few. Therefore pray earnestly to the Lord of the harvest to send out laborers into his harvest. Go your way; behold, I am sending you out as lambs in the midst of wolves" (vv. 2–3).

Jesus said to all who believe in Him and call Him Lord:

> "I tell you the truth, anyone who has faith in me will do what I have been doing. He will do even greater things than these, because I am going to the Father. And I will do whatever you ask in my name, so that the Son may bring glory to the Father. You may ask me for anything in my name, and I will do it. If you love me, you will obey what I command. And I will ask the Father, and he will give you another Counselor [the Holy Spirit] to be with you forever—the Spirit of truth. The world cannot accept him, because it neither sees him nor knows him. But you know him, for he lives with you and will be in you." (John 14:12–17)

That's what the kingdom life is about—a life I had missed for so many years. I now studied familiar Scripture with new revelation. My eyes were opened to the full gospel of Jesus—the righteousness of Christ ascribed to us through our faith in Him (Romans 5:19; 1 Corinthians 1:30; 2 Corinthians 5:21) coupled with the knowledge that all who believe in Christ are the beloved of God, set apart in advance to do greater things than Jesus did (John 14:12; Mark 16:17).

I saw how Jesus demonstrated the truth of the gospel through healing the sick and setting people free. He proclaimed the power of the gospel through physical healing, delivering them from evil spirits and prophesying truth. He told us to do the same.

My friend Michelle and I have had the privilege of praying for many people. When God heals them, we often remark, "Is there anything more fun than this? Yay, God!"

When healing doesn't come, we are disappointed but not undaunted. We never give up, and we no longer doubt God's goodness. We just pray more. To those who are not healed, we say, "Never, never, never give up! Seek prayer, inquire of the Holy Spirit if anything is impeding your healing, meditate on the goodness of God, and ask for more faith to believe you will be healed. Jesus is always faithful."

We have encountered the Holy Spirit, so we press on and celebrate God's perfect timing and His flawless will in everything. We remember that He alone does great things—the fact that He wants to do His work through us is absolutely amazing.

God's power is made perfect in our weakness; nevertheless, we have to step out courageously to see His power demonstrated and His glory made known. The seventy-two that Jesus sent out must have felt this same way when they returned to Him, as recorded in Luke 10:17–20 ESV:

The seventy-two returned with joy, saying, "Lord, even the demons are subject to us in your name!" And he said to

232

them, "I saw Satan fall like lightning from heaven. Behold, I have given you authority to tread on serpents and scorpions, and over all the power of the enemy, and nothing shall hurt you. Nevertheless, do not rejoice in this, that the spirits are subject to you, but rejoice that your names are written in heaven."

Yep. That's it right there. We get to partner with God in what He is already doing. He doesn't need us, but He chooses to work through us. There is unspeakable joy in collaborating with the Holy Spirit in everyday life and in seeing God work. As much as we celebrate His healings and the way He sets people free, we can marvel even more that our names are recorded in Jesus' book of life.

I discovered years ago that we are all called to live as reflections of the light of Christ, just as John the Baptist did. Yet we can't be true reflections if in our hearts we don't believe that we are dearly loved children of God—beloved children chosen for encounters with God as a lifestyle and not as an exception. I pray daily the Lord will use me up for His glory, release joy through me, tell me great and unsearchable things, take me on adventures with Him, and allow His glory to be all that people remember when they meet me. The gladness of my heart overflows with love for Jesus and His people.

How amazing is our God—life giver, deliverer, and miracle maker? He is the ultimate lover of our souls, and in Ephesians 2:10 He tells us that we are His handiwork, created in Christ Jesus to do the works He prepared in advance for us to do. Since the works are prepared beforehand, we can be sure that the Lord will lead, equip, and provide everything we need. I pray you will press into Him, step out and risk, and find out for yourself. Nothing else compares.

Acknowledgments

I wish to thank everyone who has been any part of my story. You know who you are, and I apologize I could not list everyone here. Without God's miraculous intervention, the support of my incredible family and friends, the prayers of so many, and the faithful editing encouragement of Janene MacIvor, Judy Morrow, Joanne Allyn, Michelle Gallina, Rose Moynier, Patty Deyermond, and Jan Kern, this project would have ceased to be. Joel Kneedler, thanks for believing in my story before I was even healed. I love how God brought everything full circle. Thanks to the team at Thomas Nelson for your unity, dedication, and humor. A special thank you to my husband, Mike, and son, Kian, and to Dr. Randy Clark for prophesying at Voice of the Apostles 2014 that I would write a book when he didn't know I already had.

About the Author

Joanne Moody is an ordained minister through the Apostolic Network of Global Awakening and certified as a Master Equipper through the Christian Healing Certification Program of Global Awakening. She is a Christian Life Coach through Western Seminary's coaching program and has a passion to see people walking in their true identity as sons and daughters of God. She leads healing teams, teaches, speaks, and trains and equips leaders and laypeople nationally and internationally in all types of ministry venues through her ministry, Agape Freedom Fighters (www.agapefreedomfighters.org). Joanne resides in Rocklin, California, and is happily married to Mike. She loves being mom to son, Kian.